"If I am going to listen to anyone address the subject of freedom and spiritual authority, I am most interested in three things: (1) How proven is the person's spirituality? (2) How consistent to the Word and the Spirit is his or her style in leading? (3) How long has this been the case? I have known Steve Fry for more than 25 years, and that is enough to prompt my urging you to read him here. He is proven and consistent, and has been so for the whole of his extensive ministry."

—**Jack W. Hayford**, president, International Foursquare
Churches; founding pastor, The Church On The Way

"Steve Fry provides an insightful and powerful look at the topic of authority and how it touches every aspect of our lives and ministry. Steve connects the dots: Fail to understand authority and you will fail to reach your full potential, as will those who follow you."

—**Tony Perkins**, president, Family Research Council

"We are living in a season where we must have a new dimension of overcoming faith. During His days of demonstrating the Father's love, Jesus acknowledged a Roman soldier as having the greatest faith in all of Israel. He cited this man as one who understood authority. In *True Freedom* Steve Fry has developed a magnificent tool to help each of us, like that soldier, become a person of greater faith. Few books tackle the subject of the power of submission like the one you are reading. This book will satisfy your heart cry for freedom, but beware—it will also rearrange the way you view all relationships!"

—**Chuck D. Pierce**, president, Glory of Zion International
Ministries; Harvest Watchman, Global Harvest Ministries

"After decades of proven ministry, Steven Fry brings yet another seasoned word to the Body of Christ. His transparency and wit make the deep topics he explores accessible to every reader. *True Freedom* is a vital resource for everyone seeking a balanced and biblical understanding of godly authority."

—**Robert Stearns**, executive director, Eagles' Wings

"Steve Fry has given us a desperately needed gift of insight about God's loving authority and the healing of human relationships. In clear, readable prose, he illuminates principles I know to be true through hard-won personal experience. I was overwhelmed with gratitude when I put down the manuscript and knew I had such a valuable tool at hand. This book will rescue families, churches, businesses, ministries and governments from all kinds of fool-ishness, pain and division. Truly this is a word in season for our generation."

—**John Dawson**, president,
Youth With A Mission International

"Years ago I was profoundly influenced by Watchman Nee's book on authority. No Christian book on this subject has affected me like Nee's until I read Steve Fry's book *True Freedom*. We desper-ately need this book to secure our future, not only as individuals but as a church and nation. Steve brilliantly crafts a clear and simple biblical theology for the challenging subject of author-ity, including its many-sided faces: boundaries, love, leadership, submission and rebellion. This book is a must-read for every member of the Body of Christ."

—**Barbara J. Yoder**, senior pastor and lead apostle,
Shekinah Christian Church

"Simply put, Steve Fry has authority to write about authority. He draws from his wide experience in both local pastoring and trans-local ministry throughout the diverse expressions of the Church, from his experience as a father and husband and from his passion for both academic theology and personal spirituality. With his characteristically engaging and persuasive style, Steve skillfully, wisely and challengingly helps us examine and understand old truths in new ways, and successfully shows us how 'authority,' once apprehended, can be personally appropriated and applied to every area of our lives. As the title suggests, this truth about authority will set you free. Highly recommended!"

—**Stuart McAlpine**, pastor,
Christ Our Shepherd Church,
Washington, D.C.

"Steve Fry's new book *True Freedom* is a fresh call to our generation to experience the blessing of true biblical authority. We live in a generation whose motto is often 'Everyone does what is right in his own eyes.' This book exposes the root issue—our bent to act independent of God—and shows us how to realign to His authority. *True Freedom* takes a fresh look at the proper use of authority that empowers people rather than controlling them. It emphasizes the need for leaders to lead a life of servanthood, living for the success of those they oversee. Steve's insights on 'the noncontrolling leader [who] lets the truth of submission be discovered within the follower rather than demanding it' is worth the price of the book. I highly recommend this book!"

—**Larry Kreider**, international director, DCFI; author

"In *True Freedom* Steve wonderfully unfolds aspects of God's nature and character that give understanding to man's quest and need for freedom and security, and how to find them. In a time of so much misunderstanding, misuse and fear concerning authority and submission, he brings refreshing answers so the believer can find freedom through biblical understanding. The truths presented in *True Freedom* are for all ages, occupations and strata. Understanding them will bring freedom to individuals as well as to our society. They are truths we desperately need today."

—**Ruth Ruibal**, president, Julio C. Ruibal Ministry;
pastor, Ekklesia Centro Cristiano, Colombia

"*True Freedom* is a masterful insight revealing how the Kingdom of God works in our midst with power, authority and integrity.

But it is not a book to be read by the fainthearted! Submission and authority are terms that our humanity rebels against, yet they are essential to embrace if we want the depth of freedom promised in Scripture. In these pages Steve Fry offers us a veritable banquet of nonnegotiable principles that are essential reading for every serious leader who honestly desires an authentic move of God in our midst today. Steve explains God's own parameters of love, authority and boundaries that reflect the very essence of His nature and that, when implemented, release godly parameters of protection, direction and correction within every level of community and society. Within these directives we discover what it means to be in alignment with the Godhead, thereby releasing what is required for lasting transformational revival. Be prepared; *True Freedom* will demand a response!"

—**The Rev. Dr. Alistair P. Petrie**, executive director,
Partnership Ministries, B.C., Canada

"America was born in rejection of authority. Although it was a proper and historically validated rejection, our 'declaration of independence' left Americans with a problematic relationship to the idea of authority. We have, in fact, never settled the issue in coherent and comprehensive sense. That ambivalence has affected our history, economics, business, politics, law, education, religion, art and approach to community.

"Steve Fry has written a powerful and illuminating book on the authority issue. Fry is a minister and Christian artist; he writes to the Church. But what he has written here is a splendid starting point for anyone choosing to grapple with the mega-issue of authority. Future American thinkers, artists and practitioners would do well to start with this book.

"Fry has obviously thought long, hard and clearly about authority, freedom and leadership. And, as is true of many profound investigations, his observations rise above intellectual indulgence; they carry the steel-on-steel ping of truth. Readers of *True Freedom* will be the beneficiaries of his long search for truth."

—**Ed Chinn**, essayist and columnist

True Freedom

What Christian Submission and Authority Look Like

Steven Fry

Chosen

a division of Baker Publishing Group
Grand Rapids, Michigan

Published by Chosen Books
A division of Baker Publishing Group
P.O. Box 6287, Grand Rapids, MI 49516-6287
www.chosenbooks.com

Printed in the United States of America

Library of Congress Cataloging-in-Publication Data
Fry, Steve, 1954–
    True freedom : what Christian submission and authority look like / Steven Fry.
       p.   cm.
    Includes bibliographical references.
    ISBN 978-0-8007-9444-6 (pbk.)
    1. Authority—Religious aspects—Christianity. 2. Submissiveness—Religious aspects—Christianity. I. Title.
BT88.F79 2008
241—dc22   2008000800

In keeping with biblical principles of creation stewardship, Baker Publishing Group advocates the responsible use of our natural resources. As a member of the Green Press Initiative, our company uses recycled paper when possible. The text paper of this book is comprised of 30% post-consumer waste.

To my three children,
Cameron, Kelsey and Caleigh,
who have each shown a deep commitment
to know God and His ways and
who are dedicated to making Him
known to their generation.

Contents

Acknowledgments

The writing of any book is certainly a team effort, and I am grateful for the many people who assisted me on this project. First, a deep expression of appreciation to Helen Lallo, who served as my executive assistant for over four years, and without whose help this book could not have been written. She has not only given me timely wisdom over and over again, but she has been a treasured friend to my wife and me.

A big thank-you to Abby Ruibal, who has served as my personal assistant over the last several months and who has contributed a great deal of time to typing and preparing this manuscript. She has gone above and beyond the call of duty many times, and I am indebted to her for her sacrifice.

I feel a profound sense of appreciation toward our local congregation, The Gate, whom my wife and I have the privilege of pastoring. They have been very gracious to let me take the time I needed to develop this book. I am especially grateful to my staff, Cindy Whitman and Aaron Weaver, who have carried a huge load during the months it has taken me to complete the book.

I am also grateful for the leaders and pastors with whom I walk in Messenger Fellowship. Your friendship and camaraderie have been a deep well from which I have drawn great joy and satisfaction.

And then to Jane Campbell, who encouraged me to take on this subject and whose expertise and advice brought my writing to a new level—a deep thanks to you. Andy Sloan, who worked with me in the final stages of editing the manuscript, has been a real gem.

Finally, I am so grateful for my wife, Nancy, who not only labors with me in pastoring the flock at The Gate but also has sacrificed perhaps more than any other person in allowing me to work the long hours needed to complete this book. She, along with my kids, Cameron, Kelsey and Caleigh, are God's sweetest gifts to me on this earth.

To say that I am grateful to Jesus would be understating the truth. I am not only thankful to Him; I am utterly dependent on Him. To be under His authority is to know the greatest freedom, and to give Him glory, the greatest joy.

1

The Root of All Wrong

It matters not how straight the gate,
How charged with punishments the scroll,
I am the master of my fate:
I am the captain of my soul.

Some of the last words
of Timothy McVeigh, quoting
William Ernest Henley's poem "Invictus"

On December 2, 1964, a fiery young radical named Mario Savio, rising star in the fledgling Free Speech Movement, fanned the flames at a sit-in at Sproul Plaza in the heart of the University of California, Berkeley. In his famous "Gears of the Machine" speech, Savio took aim at the university's governing authorities:

There's a time when the operation of the machine becomes so odious, makes you so sick at heart, that you can't take part, you can't even passively take part; and you've got to put your bodies upon the gears and upon the wheels, upon the levers, upon all the apparatus, and you've got to make it stop! And you've got to indicate to the people who run it, to the people who own it, that unless you're free, the machine will be prevented from working at all![1]

Words of a firebrand challenging the powers-that-be, yes, which no doubt sought to redress injustices in the university system. But at this moment—and many like them in the 1960s—a Pandora's box was opened, releasing a contagion of rebellion that has infected successive generations. The Free Speech Movement went national, and the mantra "question authority" was born, which became the signal slogan of a generation defined by a wholesale resistance to any boundary. Unbridled freedom was pursued and enshrined as the ultimate value.

That many social evils, not the least of which was racism, and the institutions that perpetuated them needed to be confronted is not in question. But what came with this impulse for societal reform was a carte blanche to defy the *concept and structures* of authority at every level. It was the first time since the founding of the nation that a generation *as an entire generation* attempted to overthrow the boundaries of authority. When a generation does this, it gives entry to Satan to begin systematically destroying society layer by layer.

Proverbs 22:28 says, "Do not move an ancient boundary stone set up by your forefathers." Land boundaries in ancient times were considered covenant markers. A person could not just arbitrarily move these markers in an attempt to enlarge his territory, because they represented a solemn agreement that had been made between two people. In fact, to do so invited a divine curse.

It might seem a small thing to us, simply moving a land sign a few feet, but to the ancients this was serious stuff. The reason lies in the fact that all such agreements, taken together over time, created a "society." These covenants became, over generations, the way people within a given territory related to each other. These relationships became law and, ultimately, the way "authority" was mutually experienced.

Therefore, to move a boundary stone was to violate *the whole of society*. It was not a matter of individual preference. Changing territorial ownership ripped apart a society's ability to function. The injunction in Proverbs is leveled not at those who seek to rid themselves of ancient boundary stones, but rather at those who seek merely to *move* them. Yet this was considered alarming. To violate authority, however "private" the violation might be, was to attack society—by changing the rules that had shaped how people functioned and lived together. Again, such a seemingly insignificant act was not only a matter of individual sin; it was an act against one's fellows.

I think this illustrates a broader truth. Authority is about boundaries—boundaries that have often been in place for generations. "Honor your father and mother" is a boundary stone that has cemented societies in most every culture throughout history. A teenager may think that flipping off his parents is simply an expression of his personal desire to assert his rights, but over time thousands of those acts destroy a society.

The legacy of the '60s is now being played out over the nation's relational landscape. T-shirts venomously deriding the President are national news, the f-word is basic conversational filler, relationships are cycled through and discarded like magazine subscriptions, one-third of all children born in this country are born to single parents. The list of societal decays could go on and on—trends set in motion, in large part, because authority was flaunted and boundaries ignored. There are indeed consequences when we seek to remove the ancient boundary markers.

Of course, none of this is new.

The Ultimate Root of All Problems

If we trace the problems in the world to their ultimate source, what do we find? What is the root of every social ill? Where did evil begin?

Such questions madden philosophers and defy simplistic answers. Yet as we peel back the layers of time, we ultimately find an archangel by the name of Lucifer who decided to rebel against God. But Lucifer's act of defiance is not as one-dimensional as we might first suppose. There are a couple of things about this revolt that strike me. First, I don't know that Lucifer's sin was rebellion in the full sense of the word. He did not seek to replace God or overthrow God. He simply sought to act *independent of God*. Second, when he *did* rebel, he was in a relationship with God in which he was perfectly loved by God. He was secure. Therefore, I suggest that *his action was not prompted by a love deficit.*

This leads me to two corresponding conclusions: One, the root sin of all sins is this desire to act independent of

God; and, two, the root of all problems in the universe is not a love deficit, strictly speaking, but an authority breach. As Watchman Nee observes, "To offend God's authority is a rebellion far more serious than that of offending God's holiness."[2]

The implications of this are of profound consequence. If the root of all misery goes back to this breach of authority, then understanding authority—how it is exercised, how we relate to it—is one of the most vital issues in life with which we will ever come to terms. Many assume that the root problem of the human race is a love deficit, exhibited in fear-based relationships and low self-esteem. But if the root cause of our problems is an authority breach, then our views about how we minister to people and treat human need may be radically altered.

It is axiomatic for many ministers and therapists to assume that the root problem of people is, in fact, a love deficit. And my hunch is that because we assume that this is the root, our ministry to and counseling of people is shaped along what I would call "soulish" lines. That is, when it comes to ministering to human need, we seek first to heal people's emotions: emphasizing the building of one's esteem, helping people feel good about themselves, restoring in them a sense of God's Fatherhood—that sort of thing. And all these approaches to the human condition are *right*, but may not be *root*.

I have wondered why a good many believers continue to have problems, continue to need therapy. Could it be that they—and we—are trying to address the problems by treating the soul and not the spirit? By getting people to focus on healing their wounds rather than repenting of their sins?

Now before anyone recoils at what may sound like an uncaring perspective, let me offer some very important qualifiers. First, I am *not* saying that love deficits are not critical and that wounds do not need healing. But I would suggest that a love deficit is the *consequence* of the root of independence manifest in a system of rebellion, which is the system of the world. We can be victims of this system and thus experience a potentially scarring love deficit. But the spirit of independence infects us nevertheless. Second, I am not for a moment pooh-poohing the priority of walking in honest, vulnerable relationships where the ongoing mending of one's soul, through the curative of love, sweetly massages the very real bruises of victimization.

I am simply saying that to treat humankind's ills solely along these lines is shortsighted. If the ultimate root of evil has to do with an authority breach rather than a love deficit, then the root of all roots is the spirit of independence. I would go so far as to say that the spirit or attitude of independence is the essence of pride and the root of the entire demonic system. And the only way this is dealt a deathblow is through a lifestyle of repentance, for it is in repenting that we both reaffirm God's authority and express our commitment to that authority.

To our detriment we have, in much of the Church, a narrow understanding of repentance, rarely seeing it as the key to freedom. Nevertheless—and we will look at this in greater depth later on—I suggest that it is through a lifestyle of joyous, continuous repentance that true freedom is maintained; and this repentance is the trigger point to experiencing personal peace and confidence on a regular basis.

Free Trips and Safe Places

Right here at the start we need to be honest about our uneasiness with the concept of authority. Most of us have a love-hate relationship with it. We want the safety that being properly related to authority brings, but we do not want to lose our independence in the process. No doubt this ambiguity has no small basis in our experiences. Many of us have labored under calloused employers, have been neglected by parents or have been disappointed by pastors or priests. So we want it and shun it at the same time. Nevertheless, understanding and relating to authority is a nonnegotiable of life.

James Waldroop and Timothy Butler, in their article "Managing Away Bad Habits," summarize this tension: "Most of us are ambivalent about authority. As children, for example, we often rebel against our parents even as we want to remain under their protection. . . . People like the idea of having a mentor but rebel when they actually have one."[3]

This conflict over authority recently struck me with comical force. While on a trip I decided to work out in a local gym. I was relaxing in the sauna, and a young man started a conversation with me. I do not know how we got onto the subject, but he was anxious to pontificate about the evils of government in general and our government in particular. "The only thing hierarchies do is fight power struggles within the hierarchy and against other hierarchies."

Satisfied that he had solved the problems of the world with such a succinct dismissal of authority systems, he proceeded to throw his towel on the locker room floor—right under the sign that said "Please do not leave your towels on the locker room floor.—The Management"—and walk away.

Like this man, we often chafe at authority without recognizing the benefits (in his case, a comfortable sauna in which he could throw his little hissy fit) we derive from the order authority brings. Thus, we live with an inner tension. And we feel this tension because there are two basic yet conflicting needs within us: the need to feel safe and secure *and* the need to be free.

Throughout history humankind has swung between the desire for freedom and the need for security. At present we, in American society, are acutely torn between these two forces. Since the 1960s the individual has steadily gained more autonomy, but at a fearful price—many no longer feel safe! And this feeling of being unsafe had been growing long before the collapse of the Twin Towers. The pop group Train, in their hit "Calling All Angels," paints a grim picture of a fearful society: "When kids can't play outside for fear they'll disappear . . ."

I suggest that it is because our society has bucked legitimate authority that we find ourselves dueling with this cultural angst. Of course, the moment I make this claim, legitimate concerns arise. Do we become compliant, forgoing freedoms in the name of security, and thus open ourselves up to oppression?

How can we preserve our freedom *and* maintain our security?

I suggest that it is precisely in rightly understanding authority—and most importantly, *God's* authority—that these two needs can be met. We can, in this journey called life, feel truly free but safe at the same time. *We can experience free trips and safe places.*

If we are not well anchored to God's authority, and the principles by which He releases authority to and through others, we will ever be swinging between freedom and security, ultimately producing that prototypical 21ˢᵗ century person whom we so often encounter in our society: the independent neurotic—at once stubbornly asserting his independence yet all the while feeling lost and isolated because he cannot sustain meaningful relationships (a dilemma we will explore more thoroughly in a later chapter).

Unless we understand how to walk in and walk under grace-laced authority, we will set ourselves up to be dominated and intimidated on the one hand or riddled with anxiety on the other: either pressing our boundaries past the point of sanity or swinging the other way—kowtowing to others in such a way that we lose any bearing of personal authenticity.

Caught between Two Desires

The Weimar Republic in early twentieth-century Germany offers an intriguing snapshot of what this freedom-security swing looks like in an entire culture caught in an "authority vacuum." In the aftermath of World War I, German society was seized with a reckless abandon. The strictures of war under which the people had strained were thrown off in a frenzied pursuit of freedom. Boundaries were thrown to the wind; conventional protocols were ignored; social mores were chucked; and the no-holds-barred, freedom-at-any-price, party-till-you-drop Weimar

Republic was born. It seems that the entire culture swung from a rigid authoritarianism to a roaring pursuit of liberty that was determined to push every envelope of personal freedom.

Some historians feel that it was Germany's dramatic swing from structured authority to libertinism that paved the way culturally for the Nazi takeover. For what German society came to realize was that freedom with no boundaries created a very unstable and unsafe environment. The people's hunger for freedom inevitably clashed with their need for safety. In the end safety won out, and they as a culture were quite willing to give themselves over to an authoritarianism that spawned one of the most destructive regimes ever witnessed on the human stage.

There is in all of us an ongoing struggle between these two very deep desires—freedom and security. Security implies some sort of boundaries: locked doors, fenced playgrounds, cultural conventions, constitutional laws. Boundaries engender a sense of safety. But after a while we come to chafe under boundaries like these and yearn for greater freedom. A nagging curiosity within us often prods us to explore what is beyond the locked door. What if we did not have these constitutional constraints? What if I did eat the fruit of the Tree of Knowledge of Good and Evil?

We thus find ourselves kicking at our fences, wanting to give full rein to freedom's impulses. So we break down doors, break up relationships, break away from rules—only to find ourselves lonely and insecure. All too often we then accept even more authoritarian systems . . . but find ourselves resentful of those very systems. How can these two needs—freedom and safety—ever be met?

Here, I think, is precisely why we need to understand the concept of authority. For authority, rightly understood, melds these two desires.

The Weimar Republic is not too distant from what we have experienced in our own culture since World War II. The great builders of society who led us during the war were the ones who gave us the leadership to build America in the 1950s. Though the tensions of racism and injustice were simmering just below the surface, society in the main experienced rapid growth and expansion. It was an era of expansion because it was also an era of order. Father knew best and Ward Cleaver was ever-present to give Beaver and his buddies their boundaries.

But pressure was building—a subterranean antagonism toward those boundaries, which steadily increased in the '60s. The steam of protest that began to leak through the ever-widening fissures in the great ordered world of America soon erupted into the lava flow of rebellion against all authority. As a matter of fact, what we witnessed in the '60s was the first time in the history of this nation that an entire generation—lock, stock and barrel—overthrew the boundaries of authority.

The result? We are now much "freer" than we have ever been. Freedom has become the ultimate culturally enshrined value. And where has that freedom gotten us? We can now be our own little gods in our virtual world. The Internet has increased our capacities for both good and evil beyond any conceivable imagination heretofore.

The further result? People in our culture feel less safe than ever before. And it is not just the sense of danger clutching the soul in the aftermath of 9/11. It is more vague—and thus more emotionally debilitating—than that. This feeling of being unsafe is seen in the apprehension that registers in parents when confronted with one more thing they need to monitor for the sake of their children. It registers in the worry about our borders, however predisposed we may be to treating the immigrant (legal or otherwise) with care and dignity. It registers in consumers who are faced with such a myriad of options on almost any choice that they find themselves emotionally numb.

But at least we're free.

But are we? Have we bought into the lie that says that the only way we can authentically be free is to chuck the boundaries of authority? Authentic freedom is not the license to run one's own life. It is not the preservation of limitless options. Freedom is the mastery of our beasts within. It is learning to rule our own inner person, as Scripture says in Proverbs 16:32: "He who is slow to anger is better than the mighty, and he who rules his spirit, than he who captures a city" (NASB). Authentic freedom is measured not by the assertion of our rights but by the consistency of our inward peace.

Summary

The cry for freedom echoes in every heart. But do we gain freedom simply by asserting our independence? If the root cause of the wrong in the world goes back to one being—Lucifer—attempting to act independent of God, then does it not follow that to right this wrong we need to do the opposite and realign ourselves to God's authority?

Before he asserted his independence, Lucifer was perfectly loved and thus perfectly free. I suggest that *the key to personal freedom is yielding to God's authority and the ways in which He expresses that authority.* My hope, in writing this book, is that we rightly understand authority. Why is submission to authority important to understand? When is it right to challenge authority, and how do we do that? How do we know when we are resisting legitimate authority? How does alignment to God's authority produce inner peace?

If we understand how authority works, we will be able to walk in a place of unthreatened security, joyous freedom and unshakable peace.

2

Getting It Right

Freedom is about authority. Freedom is about the willingness
of every single human being to cede to lawful authority a great
deal of discretion about what you do and how you do it.

Rudy Giuliani

If the root of all wrong in the universe is an authority breach,
then rectifying this breach becomes the ultimate issue of
life. As important as it is that we feel loved and accepted, as
important as our sense of purpose and significance may be,
our realignment to God's authority—and all of the implications contained in that—should be life's top priority.

Interestingly enough, the ultimate aim that God has for
you and me is freedom. Paul the apostle said that it was for
freedom that Christ set us free (see Galatians 5:1). If the

central issue of life is submission to God's authority, and God's ultimate aim for you and me is freedom, then it must follow that *the key to freedom is an understanding of and a realigning to God's authority*—and how the concept of authority plays out in the warp and woof of our lives.

Some years ago an experiment was conducted in which sociologists explored the playtime behaviors of schoolchildren during recess. Specifically, they wanted to see how much area in a given playground an average group of schoolkids would utilize during their play. The outcomes were telling. They found that in an unfenced area, schoolchildren would tend to huddle together and play in only a small part of the playground. But if the grounds were fenced, they found that the children would spread out and cover the entire playground right up to the fence lines.

They concluded that the fences actually provided a sense of security for the children, seemingly empowering them to cover more territory. In other words, *fences created a greater sense of freedom.* One would think that such boundaries would frustrate and inhibit kids. But the opposite appears to be true. Children without boundaries seem restrained by insecurities that actually stifle freedom.

If the concept of authority is rightly understood and applied, genuine freedom should thrive. Those playground fences were the boundaries that represented authority. Like it or not, fences are a reality, whether they take the form of stop signs on the road, IRS deadlines, chains of command or defining partnerships in a healthy marriage. Yet the kids in this experiment did not feel controlled by that "authority"; rather, they felt secure to act more freely. *Understanding authority is the key to personal freedom.*

Authority and boundaries, then, are closely related; so one of the ways we can assess our response toward the idea of "authority" is how we come to terms with boundaries in our lives. A pertinent question to ask ourselves is how we handle boundaries. Do we understand their importance and respond with grace when we bump against them? Or do we bristle, fearful that our freedoms are being curbed?

Deep within, we all know that the essence of freedom is not independence. Rather, it is fulfilling our divine design. If there is a God, and He did make us, then the freest we can ever be is when we are living fully within that design. To live within our God-authored design is to submit to a boundary. And yet this boundary results in freedom.

A tiger is freest in the wild; a golden retriever is "freest" when serving its master. For most of us, the tiger captures the essence of "freedom." Yet the retriever is just as free. Why? Because real freedom does not have to do so much with being liberated from constraints as it does fulfilling one's design. To yield to this boundary—God's design for us—is to acknowledge His authority over us, yes, but it is also to discover the satisfaction of knowing our purpose— which actually frees us to be authentic people! Therefore, we find that freedom stride as we learn how to relate rightly to authority.

The Meaning of "Authority"

Still, it appears to be a long jump from the idea of "boundaries," speaking to us as it does of limits and control, to the desirable image of "freedom." But that is because our understanding of authority has been skewed. Satan has so conditioned our thinking that, like Pavlov's dog salivating at the sound of a bell, we often react to "authority" with an almost instinctual panic of being controlled.

Psychologists have even labeled this fear. They call it *reactance*—the tendency to do the exact opposite of what is requested by a loved one or a boss. What is more, a recent study conducted by Duke University suggests that it is the psychological phenomenon of "reactance" that causes most husbands to resist doing anything their wives want. Why? Because of a deep-seated fear of being controlled.[1]

Satan has hit propaganda pay dirt with the way he has twisted the meaning of authority. For most, authority equals control. Go to most dictionaries and *authority* is defined as the right—legitimately or illegitimately—to exercise power. But that equation is light years away from God's original intention. The very word *authority* stems from the Latin word *auctus*, which pertains to creating or increasing. When someone *authors* something, that person is *creating*. When we think of the "creative process," for example, we think of *freedom*. We think of *life*.

In its purest form, authority is about creating that which gives life.

"In the beginning *God* . . ."—not some force or idea, but a personal Being—*the Life*.

"In the beginning *God created* . . ." This personal Being made more life.

This is the essence of authority. He who is Eternal Life created, authored, what He was—*life*. This is what God's "fathering" is all about. It is about His giving life and doing everything to sustain life. Whatever boundaries are required—be they moral commands, natural laws, even social systems—are required *so that we may live*. Whatever else we might believe or have experienced, authority is about perpetuating life. It is not about control, and any time we go down that road we are moving away from the Father's love.

At this point, it sounds as though we are slipping into "theory mode": talking about abstract ideas when most of us just want to be sure that God is a Father who loves us, that we don't have to be intimidated by authority figures, that there is a pathway to healing for those who have suffered injustice at the hands of those who have abused their authority.

We should and will address all of these issues. But if we want to be convinced that "authority" is the key to personal freedom, we have to be *changed in our minds about what authority is and how it is exercised.*

It is intriguing that the word *authority* is used sparingly in the Old Testament. We think that the essence of authority is power; the one who can impose his or her will has authority. But this approach to authority is not at all central to a Hebrew mindset. The Israelite would have understood authority in terms of *creation*. The original Greek use of the term had more to do with the idea of receiving permission or of having the freedom to act. In both cases the root meaning of *authority* had little to do with the use of power. If we combine the Hebrew and Greek concepts of authority, we might come to a different understanding of the word: It is the *freedom to create*. God's authority, at its core, is His freedom to create.

Authority is thus very closely tied to the concept of freedom. The reason why this is so important is that we must find an understanding and application of the concept of authority that goes to the original intent of authority in the first place, which is the maximizing of an individual's and a community's *life*—and therefore *freedom*. A right understanding of authority should produce genuine freedom in everyone. It should protect us from hurtful situations in which authority is abused; it should also release us—including leaders—into the full exercise of our gifts and the realization of our destiny. Getting to the root of the meaning of authority will help us avoid rebellion on the one hand and being controlling on the other.

Angles on "Authority"

Before going further, let's identify more precisely the ways we use the word *authority*. When we think of "authority" we often think of a person or a group possessing the power to command our compliance. This we might call *positional* authority—someone or some government having the right or power to rule over us. Some might speak of *legal* authority— the rule of law. Still others might speak of *moral* authority, which has to do with having the right to influence based on the rightness of one's character. We might even refer to *technical* authority, based on the expertise of one's skills in a given area. Some use the word *authority* in the entirely different sense of having *spiritual* authority—knowing who we as believers are in Christ and how we have been given authority over sin and demonic powers.

The word *authority* evokes varied emotions. To one, authority suggests spiritual privileges. To another, it stirs up images of hurt and abuse. Though we will touch on our spiritual authority in this book, we are dealing primarily with positional authority. How do we come under God's delegated authority without compromising our convictions? How do we handle authority given to us in ways that, in the apostle Paul's words, "build up" rather than "tear down" (see 2 Corinthians 13:10)? If we are "followers" in certain settings, how can we cultivate a submissive attitude without becoming a doormat? If we are leaders in certain settings, how do we use our authority in such a way as to inspire people to fulfill their God-given purposes? If the root of all problems stems from an initial breach of God's authority, then examining these questions is of utmost importance.

Aligning to God's authority makes sense. The payoffs when we do are rich: stronger resistance to temptation; heightened sense of personal worth; greater faith; deeper peace.

Victory over Temptation

Take temptation. Those who have not learned to align to authority will not value boundaries and will consequently find themselves more vulnerable to temptation, because they have not developed the *inward* boundaries that come from having submitted to *outward* boundaries.

Cheerfully accepting boundaries can actually create a certain addiction to holiness. Here is how this happens. When we sin, we are called to repent. If we do repent, it is in that repentance that we set up boundaries. As we live within those boundaries, we find ourselves more and more empowered to walk in personal authority, measured in peace and self-confidence. In this way we take inner territory! We find that sense of God's delight in us because we are ruling our inner man (see Proverbs 16:32). For example, when we create a new habit, we then live within that boundary for three or four days. By the time we have lived with those boundaries for several more days, we feel more excited about who we are.

That is the way that spiritual authority works! We feel good about ourselves because we are doing right—and in this way we can, by the power of the Spirit within, become addicted to the pleasure of holiness! So, aligning to authority in this case, by yielding to moral boundaries reinforced through repentance—boosts our ability to withstand temptation.

Enhanced Self-Worth

One of the most stabilizing benefits from rightly aligning to authority is the sense of personal worth we develop. Our self-esteem flourishes when we are under authority and accept boundaries. We can appreciate our *value* when we settle into our *frame*. I visited the Louvre in Paris many years ago, and purchased some prints of famous landscapes. Yet when I arrived home I stuck them in a closet and did not frame them for a long time. Of course the prints were valuable in themselves, but only I could enjoy their value until I had them matted and framed. When I finally got around to doing that, I hung them on the wall for everyone's enjoyment. As long as those prints were rolled up in little cardboard containers, they were of no use to anyone!

Likewise, our personal sense of value and worth is best realized when we are "in our frame." Paradoxically, it is as we yield to authority and accept our boundaries that we actually enhance our sense of worth. Contrarily, pursuing freedom without being under authority will, over time, destroy our sense of personal worth. You see, it is as we live in the framework of authority that a context is established for people to know how to relate to us. If people can't connect to us we will find ourselves fighting a sense of rejection that will undermine our sense of self-worth. A picture without a frame cannot be hung. A river with no banks is not navigable. Neither can a person not rightly related to authority, who bucks his boundaries, be fully appreciated.

The greater irony is that those who are loudest in demanding their freedoms become the ones most susceptible to the control of others later on. For a person without boundaries ultimately wearies of the emotional roller coaster his "freedoms" take him on. Over time, people have a harder and harder time relating to such a one. This can cause such a sense of rejection in the "free spirit" that he succumbs to far more controlling relationships than he would otherwise tolerate, because he is so desperate for relationship. Rightly aligning to authority produces an individual who can actually know the greater freedom to cultivate friendships without being controlled by them.

If people disregard authority, they will grasp for freedom yet resist boundaries, which ultimately results in personal insecurity. If they then abuse their freedom, the tendency is to ensure their security by grabbing relationships at any cost, which results in their being dishonest, saving face, even conforming to objectionable social norms that ultimately destroy their sense of self-worth because they feel they are not being genuine.

Greater Faith

Those "under authority" actually have a better picture of the authority they have. Remember the centurion's great faith in the gospel story? His faith was built on his understanding of authority. He was under authority, and he had authority. He didn't just say, "I am under authority"; and he didn't just say, "I have authority over those under me." He understood both. His was not the mindset of one controlled, who says, "I am under authority" only. You do not find any passivity, insecurity or inferiority in him. He knew that he had authority. But neither did he trumpet that point. We do not see in him any arrogance or hunger for power either.

What you see is a man rightly ordered. All people have to be under authority; and when they are, they are more trusted with handling authority. The centurion thus knew his place, and it bred within him a great sense of confidence. Being under authority increased his sense of bearing, his "authority."

The centurion's whole worldview was built on this understanding. When he came to Jesus he immediately assumed that for Jesus to be moving in authority, He was also under authority, and thus would know the same sense of "confidence" in His sphere of the miraculous that he, the centurion, knew as a Roman officer. Therefore, the centurion knew exactly how Jesus' authority was to be expressed; he did not need to draw Jesus to his house; he did not expect Jesus to meet his expectations in order to exercise His authority.

The point here is that just as the centurion's acceptance of his own authority boundaries increased his personal sense of confidence, so as we walk under authority we will increase in faith.

The Original Peace Movement

The concept of authority is about boundaries. But it is not so much about boundaries in the sense of limits as it is about *the right order of things*. To some, boundaries speak only of confinement; but they more constructively describe "right designs."

In the commercial world all kinds of manufacturing standards are established in order for products to "fit" rightly in our bigger world. For example, luggage manufacturers will not produce carry-on bags over a certain size. They are limited by a standard carry-on space in most airplanes. That limitation is not a handcuff to them—they simply recognize the "order" of why planes need to be certain sizes with certain dimensions for their carry-on space. By accepting these limitations—and not insisting on manufacturing huge carry-on bags—the luggage companies are actually "aligning to the right order of things."

The result? They sell bags, customers are resourced well, the company makes money, the employees are happy, the stockholders are content. Because the luggage companies accept "the order of things," they, at least theoretically, create a more satisfying environment for all concerned.

Authority is about right design and order. By aligning to the right order of things, we have a better shot at living satisfied, content and peaceful. And this is another reason why the issue of authority is relevant: because it touches on one of the most sought-after commodities in our society—peace.

In Isaiah 9:6–7, the Messiah is called the Prince of Peace. The term *prince* is a governmental term, and Isaiah states that the government will be on his shoulders. When Christ is in control, the result is peace. Applying this passage personally, we can say that as we yield to Christ's authority, we realize His peace. That is why Isaiah goes on to say, "There will be no end to the increase of His government or of peace" (NASB).

When we are rightly aligned to His government, His order of things, the result is peace. If we have little peace, chances are we are not rightly aligned to authority—at least somewhere. Paul picks up this theme in Colossians 3:15: "Let the peace of Christ rule in your hearts, to which indeed you were called in one body" (NASB). Inner peace is an indicator that we are rightly aligned to His authority.

It is intriguing that the Messiah is called *Prince of Peace*. Most everywhere in Scripture He is referred to as a king. Why is He called a prince in this verse? Perhaps it conveys a striking truth: God perfectly models authority within His fellowship of Father, Son and Spirit. It is as if God wants to communicate to us that though the Son is equal to the Father as deity, He is perfectly willing to be a prince under the Father's kingship in the mission of saving lost humanity. Even within God's own being, peace is fully realized because the truth of authority is perfectly lived out.

The need for peace—and the reality that most of us live stressed-out lives—hits us where we live. Everywhere we turn we confront the ways stress has altered the social landscape: a slew of stress-management techniques, programs that will help us alleviate stress, new drugs that will help us keep a lid on our anxieties. And maybe this is part of the problem—we are trying to *manage* our stress rather than eliminate it!

Much of our stress is caused by not leaning into God's design of things, His "ways." In Psalm 95 the psalmist reminds the people that their forebears' rebellion was rooted in their disregard for God's ways, resulting in the decree that they would not enter into His rest—a note that the book of

Hebrews sounds in the third and fourth chapters. Much of our anxiety is the result of not taking time to discover the ways God does things.

Ironically, one of the most rebellious icons of the '60s social revolution, Jim Morrison, lead singer of The Doors, understood that to align to authority is to be inwardly "together." "When you make your peace with authority," he said, "you become authority." In other words, when you and I align to God's authority by submitting to His delegated authorities, we tap into the original "peace movement" and cultivate an inner confidence for which we deeply hunger. That's true freedom!

3

Authority— Another Word for Love

We, like a beaten puppy, sometimes shrink away from the authority of our Father God because we assume He will be like the other authority figures in our lives. He will not. He is perfect love.

Floyd McClung, *The Father Heart of God*

At a family retreat a few years ago, I was teamed with a young leader who was there to minister to the youth while I addressed the adults. During our short time together, he told me a fascinating story from his own ministry that underscores the truth that real authority is about real love . . . and real boundaries are about real freedom.

He sponsors events in his hometown that are designed to reach teenagers. One weekend he had planned a big party, and had committed to picking up a junior high girl from her home and driving her to the event. He asked one of her friends to accompany him. When they drove into the driveway, they noticed her father watering his garden. Soon the young girl came bounding out of the door. She was provocatively dressed, this sprite of a thirteen-year-old girl, looking more like a streetwalker than a junior high student.

As she approached the car, she passed her dad who was fussing over his roses. "Bye, Dad," she said.

He looked up at her and simply responded, "Bye, honey. Have a good time!"

When she climbed into the car, she seemed distant and glum. When they got to the gymnasium where the event was being held, she excused herself to use the restroom. She showed up a few minutes later transformed. The short shorts and plunging neckline were gone. Now she was the picture of modesty, dressed in a nice pair of jeans with a top that was much less revealing.

As he continued telling me the story, he recounted that he was completely thrown by this. Was this not the little vixen dressed to kill that he had picked up just a half hour earlier? He was puzzled, so he went to her friend and asked her why the sudden transformation. She quickly responded by saying, "Oh, I know exactly what's going on. Her father doesn't love her."

She went on to say that her peers tested their parents all the time in ways like this, just to see if they provided boundaries. She explained that what this other girl was doing was seeing if her dad would love her enough to tell her to change her clothes. "Obviously," she concluded, "her father doesn't care enough to focus on her."

For these girls, boundaries were a significant part of the language of love. And that is what the Lord wants us to see. He wants to change our thinking about authority so radically that when we hear the word *boundaries,* we actually hear the word *love.* And before we go any further in our study, we need to look at two key foundations upon which any understanding of authority must be built. The first—understanding that the word *authority* is another word for love—we will consider in this chapter. The second—how to understand and walk in our authority as believers—we will explore in the next.

Healing the "Father Wound"

That the exercise of God's authority is His kiss of love to us is a hard connection to make. For many, such divine "affection" is tough to grasp because of the wounds experienced in their relationships with their earthly fathers—wounds that are very real and often go very deep.

All of us, to varying degrees, have been disappointed by our earthly dads. I have disappointed my children at times. Dads are people and we make mistakes: unfulfilled promises, not having enough time for our kids, perfectionist leanings that put undue pressure on them to perform. But for some dads those "mistakes" are misuses of authority that take the form of harsh, cutting words; or blows to the head; or serious compromises of character, such as cheating on their wives. These actions have consequences, and one of the most harmful is what they do to the minds and hearts of children.

As we grow up, our attitudes and responses to authority are significantly shaped by our experiences with our fathers. A key reason why so many have a problem with authority is because they have been mistreated and wounded by their fathers. Psychologists tell us that when this most important authority figure in our lives—our dad—has disappointed us, we consequently have a reluctance to trust authority. No doubt our earthly fathers shape us to a large degree. No doubt when we are disappointed, even damaged by an earthly father, it triggers a deep suspicion toward other authority figures.

But for those of us born anew of the Spirit, this psychological trauma need not handicap us. Just because we may have been wounded by our earthly fathers does not mean that we have to be afraid of our Father in heaven. Yet so many believers cannot seem to hurdle this barrier and rise to a rich intimacy with God as their heavenly Father. And so they engage in round after round of therapy to try to heal their "father wound" and reconcile their past images of fatherhood with Jesus' teachings on the Father's love.

That such counseling is needed—and welcomed—is not in question. But are we approaching this in the wisest way? When we become a part of God's family through faith in Christ, are we to be continually at the mercy of the images we have of our earthly father's treatment of us? Has God left us no other way than to hobble through life with our psychological handicaps, ever distrustful of authority, ever leery of relating to Him as our Father?

Consider this: Would God allow Himself to be vulnerable to the images we have of our earthly parents? Would God create a system in which we, having been spiritually reborn, have to go through years and years of inner healing because of the way our parents—especially our dads—have treated us? I cannot imagine God being at the mercy of our memories. I cannot imagine that He has not provided a way for us to be freed from such emotional weights and healed of our "father wounds" in a timely manner. I believe that God has provided, in a way and by a process that we often do not think about or understand: the power of the Holy Spirit. From the moment we come to Christ, the Holy Spirit is within us, and it is as we learn to "walk in the Spirit," as Paul says, that we are healed of our father wounds.

Healing those images of hurt caused by our earthly fathers need not come through a long process of trying to super-impose good thoughts over bad memories. We need not shy away from God as our Father. We are not at the mercy of a painful past. We do not have to keep trying to heal our father wounds. The way to a healthy concept of God as Father is to be filled with the Spirit—and that means a daily experience of His power and leading.

Walking in the Spirit Heals Our Father Wounds

In John 4, we find Jesus making a remarkable claim to an outcast woman. As she fetches water from a well, Jesus tells her that whoever would drink of the living water—speaking of the new life that is ours by the Holy Spirit—would never thirst again. Jesus is telling us that those who experience new life in Him and are thus filled with the Spirit can know a life of genuine satisfaction and contentment that can be lived in the here and now; that we don't have to carry the wounds that would otherwise emotionally cripple us; that overwhelming disappointments need not psychologically disable us; that the thirst for joy, peace, meaning and love can be quenched *forever*!

Now either what Jesus said is true or it is not. I suggest strongly that it is, and that in fact we as believers are living far beneath our blessings. Apparently, according to Jesus, the power and work of the Holy Spirit is of such a nature that it will produce in the believer—if that believer lives under the control of the Holy Spirit—a life that, while not free from sorrow and suffering, is infused with joy.

We hear such a teaching and wonder, *Can that ever be true for me?* The apostle Paul urged the churches of Galatia to "keep in step with the Spirit" (Galatians 5:25; see also verses 16, 18). And as we, too, learn this walk—cultivating a sensitivity to the Spirit's voice through worship, trusting that He is always at work whether we feel it or not, learning to listen to and obey the inner promptings of the Spirit—we will be healed of our father wounds! I would go further to suggest that we are going to heal our father wounds not by focusing on our father wounds, but by walking in the Spirit!

Still, we ask ourselves how this can be. We have to drink—and keep on drinking—that living water. And this is part of what Paul meant when he exhorted the Ephesians to "be filled with the Spirit" (Ephesians 5:18). A closer look at the original meaning of this verse renders a better translation: "Be continually being Spirit-controlled." By coming under the authority of the Holy Spirit in our daily lives, we will quickly grow in our affection for God as our Father, and we will learn to be at peace with authorities in our lives.

Again, trying to heal our father wounds may in fact *not* heal our father wounds. Instead, the Lord invites us to forget about those hurts and start accessing the power of the Spirit (who, by the way, will empower us to forgive and keep on forgiving those who have caused us pain). I suggest that *this* is the way God intends for us to discover the riches of His Fathering love—by learning to walk in and lean into the Spirit.

Paul knew this to be the key to intimacy with the Father, and it is why he cheered the Roman Christians with the truth that we have been given the Spirit of sonship, whereby we can cry, "*Abba*, Father" (Romans 8:15).[1] In our day that would be like crying out, "Papa God." Paul is saying that we *now* have that privilege—and that if we recognize how the Spirit works in our lives, we *will* feel like God's treasured children.

Of course, we are God's children from the second we surrender to Christ, but the key to *feeling* that we are His children is learning to yield to the Spirit's control. For one of the hallmarks of Christ's very nature is His constant yearning after the Father. That yearning is now a part of your nature— if the Spirit lives within you. And from the moment we are spiritually reborn, the Spirit begins not only healing us of father wounds but also softening our distrust of authority.

Paul draws a very specific connection between our sense of being "sons"—which, in Paul's use of the term, includes both believing men and women as heirs of the Father—and being led by the Spirit. He goes on to say that we have not received a spirit that enslaves us again to fear, but we have received the Spirit of sonship, or adoption, and thereby this "*Abba*, Father" cry becomes our own. Now of course we are not just legally adopted; we are born of His Spirit. We are in a sense genetically His, as Paul Billheimer says, not just legally His.[2] And yet the fact that the apostle Paul uses the legal term *adoption* is very significant. He wants to convey that God is not *obligated* to love because we are His and He can do no else; God has *chosen* us as if we were orphaned in an alien world. To adopt us means that He has selected us to be His own!

Again, God has not left Himself at the mercy of our painful memories. We can begin walking in victory over the hurts caused by our fathers by making it our life focus to yield to the Holy Spirit's control.

But to be under His control we must be ready to hear Him say no.

When God Says No

I am a writer of songs and books. I have original manuscripts of songs I wrote when I was fourteen. I have taken pains to preserve them through several moves. I have put them in specially marked boxes and have been careful not to lend them out. I also have a number of cassette tapes on which I have recorded original melodies and songs and which I have carefully preserved. My kids—who all play the piano—know not to tamper with my tapes, lest they inadvertently damage or record over one of them.

Why have I been so precise about these "boundaries"? Because I have authored something that I feel is so valuable as to be irreplaceable. I am not motivated to set these boundaries because I enjoy power or want to control those around me. I am motivated by a keen desire to preserve what I have authored.

God has "authored" you and me. His love is so intense that He sets laws in place and establishes consequences when those laws are violated. Why? Just as I do not want my recordings to be erased and recorded over, so God does not want you and me to be destroyed. Authority is not about controlling, but preserving what has been created. So even when God says no, it really is His yes.

Of course, nobody likes to be told no. Even though we may know that it is for our best, it stings a little when someone legitimately blocks our desires—especially if the one doing the telling is an authority figure. People who tell other people no can candy-wrap it in five—or five hundred—love languages, and still it will not go down easily.

As a teenager, I would sit there and listen to my parents tell me why the boundaries (read "screws") they were putting on me were because they loved me. It sounded like a lot of spin-doctoring to me, like they just enjoyed the therapy they derived from bossing a helpless youth around. "Son, it hurts us more to say no here than it does for you to have to hear it." Who were they kidding?

I fought my personal Waterloo on this issue when I was about eight years old. My dad pastored in Southern California, and during most winters we went to Palm Springs for a few days to escape the frigid temperatures of Los Angeles. (Yeah, right! But it was cold to us!) We always stayed at a little motel called The Sands. I used to love going there because the motel had, so they claimed, an Olympic-size pool—with a high dive no less! (Of course, this was in the days before lawsuits had become the economic force driving universal economies from here to Mars.)

At any rate, year after year I just *looked* at the high dive, content to experience my thrill on the one-meter board. But I would watch others take the plunge from the safety of the shallow side, thinking maybe I would one day have the courage to climb that ladder and jump myself.

I guess something happened when I turned eight. I either gained confidence or lost sense. (When you are growing up you never know quite which it is.) This time, when we pulled up to The Sands and I raced off to the pool, that high dive did not look so high. *I can jump from this thing,* I mused to myself. So like greased lightning I ran to the room, put on my trunks and ran back to the pool to begin my assault on Mount Everest.

My mom was sitting poolside, sunning herself, and as I careened past her I shouted, "I'm divin' off the high dive, Mom! Watch me!"

This was big news to her. Her chickenhearted kid was showing some moxie. So she lowered her sunglasses and fixed her gaze on me, grateful that I would now be able to join the ranks of men. She knew that having the courage to jump off would instill in me a new level of confidence—which, as a nerdy little pup with black-rimmed glasses, was becoming an increasingly needed commodity.

I started my climb . . . which took longer than I thought. I got to the top and inched my way toward the edge of the board. I peeked down. *It's a mile drop!* I said to myself. What had looked to be but a few feet from below seemed like the top of the Empire State Building now. There was no way I was going to jump! I could just see myself landing on the water with the most colossal belly flop ever witnessed in the history of aquatic sports, my stomach bursting on impact and bits of me being sprayed all over the place.

Well, that just could not happen; I needed to protect the motel's property. So I proceeded to back off the board and climb back down the stairs.

Of course, Mom had been keenly observing all of this. As I started climbing back down the stairs, with a calm resolve in her voice she called out to me, "If you climb down those stairs and don't jump, I'm going to spank you."

What was I hearing? My mother, the one who brought me into this world, the one who would nestle me close when I bruised my shin, the one committed to—and licensed by God to—*protect and defend me*, was saying *what*? She was telling me, basically, that I could *not* back down from that dive and that if I did there would be consequences (which meant we were going on a "wailing expedition").

I was incredulous! All I was trying to do was preserve the life of her firstborn son. And she had the audacity to threaten me with a spanking? It did not make sense. But there I was: stuck on the high dive, with a growing line of impatient people urging me to jump. It was getting desperate. I was alone—unable to call my lawyer. It was either die by jumping or die by the hand of my mother.

I inched to the edge once again, peered over the board—and shuddered. But I knew I was going to have to jump. So I closed my eyes and took the plunge. It seemed like an eternity before I creased the water. And when I did, it felt like I had submerged clear to the other side of the world.

But all at once I surfaced—*alive! Breathing! I had beaten the board! I had taken the plunge, and survived.* Suddenly I was no longer a skinny little eight-year-old. I was now a *macho* eight-year-old. And for the rest of the day I jumped off, even dove off, that diving board. My confidence probably took the single largest one-time leap of my life that day at The Sands.

Was my mother being cruel or controlling when she told me, "No, you cannot come down off that board"? Looking back on this whole episode, I realize that her no was the most loving thing she could have said. For she had seen how I had let other boys at school pick on me; she knew that I suffered from the self-image of being a wimp. And she knew, that day at The Sands, that if I had not followed through with my choice to dive off that high dive I would have felt like an even greater wimp. She never forced me to climb that ladder, mind you, but once I did she knew that she had to make sure I followed through with my choice. Her apparent rigidity was the most loving thing she could have done. She knew that if I jumped it would make a new boy out of me—which it did!

Her no was the language of love at that moment.

It is hard for us to see this sometimes. But this is how God works with us. He has given us *boundaries* in His Word. He has delegated His authority in varying degrees to other people and institutions, such as civil governments, and expects us to align to those authorities. To us this might smack of control and seem to threaten our freedom. But if we understand—and, yes, even submit to—the authorities God has ordained, then we will experience what that eight-year-old did when he took the plunge: an inner confidence we have never known before. It is in submitting to God's authority—and the boundaries that come with that—that we realize *true* freedom.

4

Living in Our Authority

I have become convinced . . . that the enemy's primary area
of attack is our self-image. He does not want us to discover
who we are.

Charles Kraft, *I Give You Authority*

Understanding that God's authority is an expression of His
love is bedrock if we are to align well to authority. But there
is a second foundational truth we need to grasp before we
go on, and that is this: *To be able to submit to authority
with grace, we must first recognize the authority we have in
Christ!*

One of the reasons so many Christians have a problem
submitting to authority is that they don't realize—and walk
in—their authority as believers. That has to come first. If

we are securely grounded in God's love, and know who we are in Christ, then being under someone's authority is not threatening.

Young David is a case in point. In 1 Samuel 16, the newly anointed future king of Israel finds himself in the employ of the present king, who has not only compromised himself spiritually but can no longer hear from God. Saul was a mixture of self-interest, jealousy, fear and guilt—his soul torn by the nagging regret of knowing that his compromises had cost him his throne and his relationship with God. And this was David's mentor for a season, arranged in full by a loving God!

Most of us would question if it could ever be in God's will to put us in a situation in which we would have to submit to a compromised leader. Not once do we find David miffed at God for doing so. When Saul attacks him, God protects him. When it becomes unbearable, God releases him. David's example shows us that we can be under compromised leaders and not be harmed. David's call was never threatened, his destiny never jeopardized. And this should allay our own apprehensions about submission to authority: *There is no Saul that can thwart your call.*

But what David possessed that many of us lack is a sense of *inward* spiritual authority. He knew who he was in God and had grown in his confidence in God. And this is the second key foundation to aligning to authority.

Walking In, Walking Under

Before we explore the benefits of being rightly aligned to authorities in our lives, we need to fine-tune some important assumptions. First, we need to make a distinction between walking *in* authority and walking *under* authority. By walking *in* authority I do not mean functioning as an authority over someone else. Rather, I am referring to that *inner* authority that Proverbs 16:32 (NASB) describes when it says that "he who rules his spirit" is better than "he who captures a city." In Galatians 5:22–23, Paul lists the nine fruit of the Spirit and names self-control last—almost to suggest that this quality sums up the other eight.

Therefore, to walk *in* authority has to do with something *inside*: a posture of restful confidence, being so certain about who we are and the pathway we are to walk that we cannot be easily thrown off our axis. "Authority" begins with understanding who we are. And who we are is God's children. To walk *in* authority is to recognize the sense of place and status that are ours as children of God. *Authority is inseparable from identity.*

For example, my "authority" as a teenager poised to obtain a driver's permit was recognized in part because I shared a last name with parents who agreed to meet certain obligations on my behalf. My authority to drive was given only because my identity was recognized and accepted. Had I, as a fifteen-year-old, tried to claim authority without showing that my identity was grounded in another—namely my parents—I would not have been allowed to drive.

Knowing who we are in Christ, as children of our heavenly Father, enables us then to "rule" our emotions with genuine zest. A young driver who has any smarts knows that the privilege of driving is maintained only as the rules are followed. At one point he may want to get angry with another driver and ram his bumper, but he controls his impulses to do so.

Why? Because of the privileges he now has—privileges that stem directly from his recognized identity, which in part released him with the authority to drive in the first place.

Thus, to walk *in* authority means we first recognize and celebrate our new identity and the privileges that are now ours because of that identity, which in turn motivates us to exercise self-control over our emotions. In the classic *Ben-Hur*, Judah Ben-Hur is adopted by the Roman consul, Quintus Arrius, and receives a ring that marks his new identity. At that point, because his identity has been changed, he possesses the authority and privileges of a Roman citizen. Once adopted, his authority is not derived from tests he has passed, successes he has notched or experiences he has endured. It comes from a new identity.

So it is with us as God's children. We can know an inner authority that flows from the simple fact that we belong to Christ, and therefore we need not fear what others— even we ourselves—may do to us. This leads to a second key assumption.

This inner authority must first be cultivated within us before we can function well under someone else's authority. In other words, we must know what it means to walk *in* authority before we can walk graciously *under* authority. For if we have understood our *identity*, then those in authority over us are no longer a threat. Fear of authority no longer need shape our emotions.

The young driver with the learner's permit is not shaken when a patrolman passes him. As long as the youngster stays within certain boundaries, he not only continues to exercise his privileges but also knows protection from any abusive use of authority. If the officer were to pull him over for a minor offense and misuse his authority by unduly reaming him out, the young driver may be temporarily shaken, but his confidence is not robbed. He knows he still has the last name of his parents and that they will protect him and nurture his sense of self-confidence.

If we are walking in authority, we are actually freer to walk under someone else's authority. Conversely, if we chafe under someone else's authority, it may indicate that we are not walking *in* authority ourselves, with the sense of status and privilege that are ours as children of the King.

Once we get this right we can then better appreciate how understanding and yielding to authority meets two primary needs in the human heart. The first is that when we rightly walk in and walk under authority, we will find the right balance between safety and freedom. The second is the inner rest we can realize when, by understanding authority correctly, we have relinquished control over our lives and the lives of others.

In other words, rightly aligning to and applying the concepts of authority result in *freedom and rest*, two of the deepest needs pulsing in the human soul. It seems ironic that *authority*—a concept so often associated with control and even abuse—is actually a vital key to release, peace and inner confidence.

Walking in Our Authority Brings Peace

My wife, Nancy, came to me once expressing how freeing it was for her to "submit" to my authority as her husband. The word *authority* is not a loaded term in our marriage. We are not just partners, but understand that there is a dynamic co-equality between us. We are both valuable. We make decisions together; we try to listen to each other well. But if a decision *has* to be made—for the sake of the kids, for example—and we are not quite on the same page, she allows me to then make the decision. For her, that place of deferring to my headship is freeing because it absolves her of carrying the emotional weight of the decision's outcomes.

When we walk *in* authority, then relinquishing control is easier. There is actually a freedom that comes when we can *legitimately* release responsibility. The truth is that we carry responsibilities that are not ours to carry. When we resist legitimate authorities in our lives we are actually assuming their responsibilities—burdens that we have no grace to bear. To "buck" authority is to claim *our* right to *their* function. Why would we want to do that?

Each member of my body has its rightful place and carries an "authority," if you will, appropriate to its function. My brain has an "authority" to think, my heart an "authority" to pump life-giving blood. The heart may be "under" the brain, which functions as the stimulant to the heart's actions. But the brain is dependent on the heart to keep it supplied with blood so it *can* continue to function in its proper place—its *boundary*—as the stimulant to the heart.

I am glad my heart and brain do not have any "authority" problems, trying to usurp each other's functions. There is an order and sequence to their co-functioning, but at the end of the day they truly are interdependent.

You may be the "heart" to someone else's "brain" in a given organization or relationship. But understanding your value as a "heart" allows you to respond rightly to a leader—or, as in my wife's case, a husband—not only in a manner free from fear, but in a lifestyle unencumbered by assuming inordinate responsibilities and attempting to control your world.

Our ease with authority is determined, in large part, by how clearly we know who we are—our *identity*. But we settle *that* not by trying to find ourselves, but rather by knowing who we are in Christ.

Being "in Christ"

The grounds of our authority are obviously not in our circumstances but in our relationship to God. Our circumstances might tell us that we are weak. Our circumstances might even make us feel disqualified, especially if we feel that we have failed God. But we need to remember that our authority as believers to walk in a place of overcoming faith is grounded not in our acts of righteousness but in the fact that we are "in Christ."

The truth of being in Christ was foundational to the apostle Paul's theology. He uses the phrase "in Christ" more than eighty times in his letters (in addition to frequent usage of comparable phrases, such as "in Him"). But what exactly does that mean? It is very hard for us to get our arms around this concept because we are so shaped by what we see and sense in the empirical world. I understand when I am "in my house," since I can see that locale and it registers with me when I am inside or outside. But the idea of being "in Christ" is harder to grasp. Are we "literally" in that location called Christ? There are three ways we can look at this.

Being in the Father's "Will." First, we can be "in something" without it having to be a specific site. For example, someone might be listed in his father's will. That person does not live in the will as he would live in his house, but we understand the meaning of being "in someone's will." It means that a covenant has been established that confers rights, privileges and resources upon the heir, which belong to the heir unequivocally once the father dies. For people to say they are in someone's will means that they have the privileges of accessing the bequeather's resources promised them. Of course, the one making the will has to die before the inheritance can be claimed (see Hebrews 9:15–17).

But God has already died in the Person of His Son! So we are heirs who are already receiving our inheritance, and it began with receiving the Holy Spirit (see Ephesians 1:13–14). He is our *first inheritance*, our *deposit*. The nature of the first installment is of an *inner* quality that Paul describes in Galatians 4:6: The Spirit is constantly yearning for the Father. This inner yearning is now ours! We can know the inner "authority"—in other words, *the confidence*—that we are *constantly* in the Father's grasp.

The Father's will is the Father's *will*. That is, His purpose for you is the inheritance He has given you. A will cannot be violated by any other power, including the power of the state. It is inviolable. God's will (purpose) is His will (testament). He wants you and me to know our privileges as sons and daughters.

In sum, this is one way we can look at the idea of being "in Christ." We are named in the will and it is binding. Someone's leaving an heir a million dollars may not agree exactly with the way the heir will spend that million dollars. That is the risk taken; and in a sense the Lord has taken a risk with us. He has chosen to give us His name and all the rights of that name. The use of our privileges is not dependent on whether we feel righteous one day or not righteous the next. One might object on the grounds that such a view leads to moral compromise. But that is why it is the *Holy* Spirit who lives in us. His indwelling guarantees that the will's provisions are met. That is why the Spirit is referred to as "a deposit guaranteeing our inheritance" (Ephesians 1:14); He will work in us to make sure the qualifications of holiness are met in order for the privileges to be accessed.

We cannot lose! God confers full rights and privileges on His children, then sets it up where *He* ensures that all the provisions of the will are met. So when we say we are "in Christ," we are *in*!

Acting Securely within a Sphere of Authority. Consider the truth of being "in Christ" from another angle. Let's say you buy and sell properties; you are a broker. When asked what you do, you say, "I'm in real estate"—which means you have authority to do certain things within that particular sphere. This is not an authority that is dependent on your emotions. If you are up one day and despondent the next, your authority as a real estate agent does not change. The way you *handle* your authority may change—for instance, allowing depression to rob you of motivation—but your authority does not change. You are "in real estate" whether your emotions are positive or not.

Sometimes an agent will write a good contract, sometimes she will not. But even the quality of her work does not ultimately affect her authority as an agent. She is still "in real estate." "Well, then, the agent's performance means nothing! Where is the accountability?" If she performs at a subpar level, the pinch is felt as her pool of customers grows smaller. But then the question is not one of *losing* her authority but rather of *handling* that authority well. Character issues compromise our *use* of authority, but they do not cause that authority to be rescinded.

This may be where believers make a mistake in understanding their authority in Christ. At the point of failure they can feel they have *lost* authority. The devil makes them think they are disqualified. So they stop standing on who they are as children of God and claiming the privileges they have as His children.

Being Actually Present in Christ. There is yet another way to look at this, which actually comes closer to the idea of being in a location. Consider this: When Jesus Christ walked the earth, was God fully manifest in Him? We would, of course, say yes; as the Son of God, God was fully present in Christ. "Son of God" was one of Christ's two "Sonship" titles, and this one states the fact that the fullness of deity was in Him.

But do we have a grasp of the other title of Christ? He was not just the Son of God, but also the *Son of Man*. He preferred, in fact, to use this designation. We have a handle on God's full divinity in Christ. Do we have a handle on *our* full humanity in Christ? As God was fully Himself in the man Christ Jesus, so do we comprehend that now *we are fully present in Christ*?

What God intended for un-fallen man to be, *we now are* in Christ. Was there a part of God in Christ? No, the fullness of God was in Christ. Is there just a part of me in Christ now? No, *I am fully in Christ now*. When Christ was on earth, was God present as a *potential power* in Him? Or present as an *idea* in Christ? No, God's actual being was in Christ, the perfect intermingling of the Persons of the Father and Son. The flip side is true of Christ as Son of Man. He contains my full person perfectly within Himself in the heavenlies. His perfection is now mine. *I am as close to God as Christ is at the right hand of the Father, for I am as in Christ now as God was when Jesus walked Galilee's shores.*

Maybe we can come at this another way. When we speak of Christ coming to earth as Son of God, we speak of the *incarnation.* Something like a reverse of that has happened with *us* in Christ. Now Christ as Son of Man has gone to the Father, and as God came to earth in Christ, now we have gone to heaven in Christ. *This means that we will never be more present to the Father than we are right now in Christ!* Our being "in Christ" is more than just a legal status. He *represents us* (a doctrine called "federalism"), yes, but it is more than just in a symbolic or figurative sense. We are as present to God in Christ now as God was to humanity in Christ then.

This should lead us to three states of mind: a profound sense of security and confidence, a profound sensitivity to sin and a profound lifestyle of repentance. These are profound because if I am in Christ, *then I will always have a sense of who I am and what I need to do at any given point.* Truth and direction will not be hidden from me. God does not play cat and mouse with us. Paul says that we truly have the mind of Christ (see 1 Corinthians 2:16), which means that His mind is always present to us—as long as our hearts stay in a posture of humble dependence on Him.

By being "in Christ" we are stocked with benefits. First, *we will not lack confidence.* When Adam and Eve sinned, their eyes were both opened and closed. They were naked before they sinned, but the glory of God "covered" them and they did not *see* that they were naked. But when they sinned their eyes were opened to their nakedness *and* their lack; that is why they covered themselves with fig leaves. Their eyes were closed to that covering of God's glory.

When we know our position in Christ, we are reopening our eyes to the covering of glory that Adam and Eve knew. No wonder Paul says that we, with unveiled faces, reflect the Lord's glory (see 2 Corinthians 3:18)! The only posture that dims our awareness of who we are is when we "see" in the way that Eve saw. She saw that the fruit was desirable for wisdom—she tasted of her natural mind for the first time, and stopped leaning in humility on the Lord.

Now we might say, "Well, if I am in Christ, whatever I think is right." Yes, provided that we are walking in constant humility and trust. The process of blinding ourselves is always present whenever pride is present. And pride often begins, as it did in Eve, with the natural mind—including *our natural inclination toward justice that says that when we fail we must pay for it somehow.* But we need to stand in faith against our natural mind *here* as much as anywhere. Our natural mind says we must re-earn our authority in Christ. The mind of the Spirit says *we still have our authority in Christ and we simply need to "turn around" again—which is why repentance is such a freeing concept.*

Again, this is the revolutionary shift in thinking that occurs when we see being "in Christ" as being *actually and spiritually present in Christ at the right hand of the Father.*

Just as the Father expresses and experiences perfect love for us through Christ, so now we express perfect confidence and experience perfect security because we are in Christ also.

Second, *we will not lack spiritual sensitivity*. When I know who I am in Christ I should never be afraid of moving in confidence or of resting in my security, which means never being afraid to step out in faith or in prayer because of wondering if I am disqualified. If I am truly in Christ, then I will be even that much more sensitive to sin, because I will be as much in God's presence as Jesus is. Again, if we are in Christ, *then* we are in His presence—which paradoxically means that I should be as acutely aware of my sin as I am of my confidence.

Third, *we will persevere in prayer*. In fact, the motivation for me to persevere in prayer should be the reality that I am completely and fully in Christ. Here is where I think we sometimes fail in understanding just what kind of confidence we have in Christ. For it is not an instantaneous "name it and claim it" kind of thing. If Jesus Himself constantly makes intercession for us and never stops praying for us, then—being in Christ—we have the same privilege of praying and keeping on praying, seeking and keeping on seeking. The grounds for persevering prayer is the fact that we are complete and full *in residence in Christ*. So, for example, if I am sick I keep on praying for healing and I do not give up. The healing part is God's business, but the persevering prayer part is mine!

Think about the fact that Christ has been praying for you and me continuously. The Word says that He ever lives to make intercession for us. Have all of Christ's prayers for you and me been answered? Well, not in my life anyway, because

I am still contending with some of the things that the Lord does not want me to contend with—like worry. But He does not stop praying for me! Our approach to prayer should be the same. If Christ's prayers are not immediately answered, then neither should we be impatient if our prayers are not immediately answered.

Fourth, *we will not fear being "under" God's delegated authorities*. The fact that we are fully in Christ is the grounds for our security. Therefore, we can ultimately and utterly feel secure, no matter what chain of command or submission scenario in which we find ourselves.

Fifth, *we can know God's power in us to resist pride*. The reason God resists the proud is not just because He is personally offended by pride. In reality, He is offended by pride because it keeps us from our full authority and security in Christ—and thus from fullness of joy!

5

The Source of Authority

Man, proud man
Dressed in a little brief authority . . .
Plays such fantastic tricks before high heaven
As make the angels weep.

William Shakespeare

We have already seen how taking our cues from God about authority changes our thinking about authority—that it is fundamentally not about *control*, but rather about *creation*. God "authors." And everything He does—and the boundaries He establishes—is all about preserving what He authors. If we want to undergo the kind of mind shift in which when we hear the word *authority* we hear the word *love*, and in which we find true freedom, we need to reflect more deeply on God's character and nature. In other words, we have to do some theology.

The mere mention of the word *theology* summons images of dour theologians poring over dusty tomes that no sane person would ever understand, let alone read. But before you and I reach for our TiVo controls or check our minds at our favorite website, we need to remind ourselves of something. We Americans are a very pragmatic lot. We want to know *how* to do things, and we want to understand and do them *quickly*! In things mechanical, well, we can usually learn the minimum and then call for the specialists when our car does not run or our DVD player goes on the blink. But if this is our approach to life issues like values or relationships, this pragmatism can cost us dearly.

Because we have been weaned on a diet of immediacy, in which our aim is quick results, we often do not do the necessary homework that would enable us to apply a concept thoroughly. By not knowing *why* we ought to align ourselves to God's patterns and ways of authority, we may find ourselves caught in this inner tension of wanting God's love but resisting His ways. We may want to please the Lord, but we find ourselves fighting unnecessary battles of rebellion within. This is why doing theology is a good thing. Theology is not so much about the "hows" as the "whys." Understanding why something is the way it is may sound like a tedious waste of time, but in the long run it anchors us to solid reasons for responding rightly to God even when we may not feel like it.

So, what is God like in His nature, and what conclusions about "authority" and even "leadership" might we draw from who He is? And what is it about His nature that assures us that His authority is based in love?

The Trinity: The Proof of Love

When speaking of God we often use two different words: *character* and *nature*. His character, we might say, is who He is *morally*. He is love, He is merciful, He is truth and so on. His nature is what He is *in His eternal essence.* He is omnipotent, omniscient and all the other $100,000 words that describe His "otherness." Another way to look at these two facets of God's being is that His character is that to which the Holy Spirit is conforming us—so that we are people of love, truth and goodness. God's nature is His "stuff"—that part of God we will *never* become, nor were we ever intended to become. It is what makes God, God.

Yet His nature models to us eternal truth. The way God *is* shapes, or should shape, all that we are. And perhaps the core of His nature is that He is one being eternally expressed in three Persons, that He is a Trinity. Does the fact that God is a perfect communion of Father, Son and Spirit have any bearing on our understanding of authority? If God's nature and character are the basis of *all* reality, then it stands to reason that this is the place to begin to construct an accurate view of authority.

If God's authority flows from who He is, then His nature as a "communion of three Persons" becomes relevant. Oftentimes when we hear terms—like "the Trinity"—that point to thick theological concepts, we mentally turn off. These are mysteries with which we would rather not grapple. But understanding God as a communion of Persons becomes extremely important when it comes to understanding how authority works.

The Trinity will always be something of a mystery, although we need not hide behind a veil of ignorance and call it "faith." We can understand something of the Trinity, and one of the most satisfying aspects of the tri-unity of God is that it verifies the eternity of love! While we always must be wary of any hint of tritheism (the idea of three Gods), God is nevertheless a plurality of persons, even as He is a singularity of being. And the very nature of His tri-unity—that He is three Persons—gives us a firm basis to know that love has always existed. We can know that God is love, as the apostle John says in 1 John 4:8, not just because He says He is, but because His very nature substantiates it.

In order to grasp this, it might be helpful to compare biblical Christianity with Islam. In Islam God is understood as one divine person, Allah. God is perceived as strictly unitary, rather than as a dynamic plurality eternally abiding in a comprehensive unity. Muhammad felt this to be a higher revelation than Christianity. But is it? If there was indeed a time before all creation when there was no one but Allah, how does one know if Allah was good? How does one know if Allah was love? All we have is Allah's word; there is nothing intrinsic in his nature that would verify the eternity of love.

Love, by definition, must have an object to be verified. Before anything was created—if one takes the Muslim position to its logical conclusion—Allah "existed" with no one "other" to love. For all we know, a singular deity like Allah could be capricious, arbitrary, even cruel. A Muslim's fatalism is merely the extension of his perception of God. For since there is no basis for morality within Allah's nature, love cannot be validated; and if we cannot be certain of

God's character, we cannot be certain of anything! Hence fatalism is the only coping mechanism to which a Muslim can resort.

As Trinity, however, the Father has always loved the Son and the Spirit; the Son has always loved the Father and the Spirit; the Spirit has always responded in like manner to the Father and the Son. It is pretty mind-bending to realize that God the Father has never thought of Himself exclusively in terms of Himself. He has always thought of the other two Persons within the Godhead—pure unity expressed in vibrant plurality. Such essence set against the backdrop of my behavior exposes the sickness of my self-absorption. The Godhead as the Godhead gives me an anchor that assures me of the eternity of love. I can say that love has always been, for it is the basis of God's nature. Therefore, God has never been capricious; for within the Trinity each Person has been the object of the others' love and adoration!

Relishing in this truth, Richard of St. Victor, a twelfth-century cleric, exclaims:

> If there was only one person in the divinity, that one person could certainly not have anyone with whom he could share the riches of his greatness. . . . Only someone who has a partner and a loved one in that love that has been shown to him possesses the sweetness of such delights. . . . Such a sharing of love cannot exist except among no less than three persons.[1]

We may describe God's character as compassionate, just, merciful. Yet, while these are indeed perfect words with which to describe Him, love is at the *core* of His very being.

Thus, *everything God does is because of love,* including the ways He exercises authority—which means that when God says no it is meant to preserve our life.

The Trinity and the Definition of Authority

What constitutes "authority"? That is, on what grounds does anyone have the right to exercise authority? Is authority based on power? Does the person who has power have authority, since he has the means of enforcing his will? Is authority based on mutual consensus? Does authority "emerge" within a group based on a sort of social contract which that group makes with each other? Is there a universal set of laws that determines who has the right to exercise authority?

The challenge with each of these approaches to authority is that authority becomes relative to the situation. Power brokers change. Social contracts can change. What may be proper behavior in a group in one season can dramatically change in another season. And if there is a universal law upon which authority is based, such as the law of love that says, "Do unto others as you would have them do unto you," who determines the precise definition of *love*? That can change from culture to culture. To lie and betray people is deemed to be wrong in a Judeo-Christian culture. But in certain tribal cultures betrayal is seen as the ultimate act of manhood and is supremely honored.

The question of what constitutes authority has never been more acute than now. In today's world—in which we are seeing an unprecedented empowering of the individual—institutions and systems that have been utilitarian (in which leaders use people as resources for their aims and goals) or unduly hierarchical (in which followers have little or no voice and are not valued in the same way as leaders) have been coming under more and more scrutiny. The Church herself has come under the microscope; there is a palpable restlessness in her ranks as to the ways authority is handled and leadership is exercised.

The tri-unity of God may offer us some insights to these sensitive issues. And while drawing comparisons between God's nature and the way we "do church" is bound to be inexact at points, it is worth exploring. For if we ground any truth in the character and nature of God, we will be more motivated to live in that truth. So seeing how authority is modeled within the Community of Three may help us clear up some misconceptions about authority and how it is to be exercised—so that when we hear the word *authority*, we *are* hearing the words *love* and *freedom*.[2]

What's the Big Deal about the Trinity?

How we understand the relations between the three divine Persons has a direct bearing on our perception of authority. If, for example, we conceive the Son as eternally subordinate to the Father, we may be more likely to favor hierarchical leadership structures, in which power is vested more heavily in one person. If we see the Trinity as being strictly a co-equal relationship of the three Persons, we may favor more democratic systems of leadership and government, in which power is more equally distributed. And of course, as is usually the case, one size does not fit all. These two approaches to understanding the Trinity are not contradictory. In fact, both views have scriptural support and have some practical application for us.

So how has the Church understood the Trinity over the centuries?

The literature of some of the early Church fathers presents us with divergent views as to the precise ways the three Persons in the Godhead interrelate. Some saw distinct functions and roles in God's being, but tended to stress the equality of the Persons.[3] Others saw a more defined hierarchy in God's being that stresses the supremacy of the Father.[4] This discussion has come to be known as the "monarchy" issue. The word comes from the Greek root words *mono*, meaning "one," and *arché*, meaning "authority." So the monarchy issue has to do with "who has the authority?"

When the earliest of the Church fathers focused on the inner relations of the Father, Son and Spirit, they were primarily interested in how God was accomplishing our salvation. When looking at the Godhead through these lenses, it is quite appropriate to see how the three Persons function in a *hierarchical* sense. For example, we see the Son as "subordinate" to the Father, who did nothing except what He saw the Father doing (see John 5:19–20). We see the Father "sending" the Holy Spirit in the name of the Son (see John 14:26; 15:26)—again implying a kind of "order" to their relationships. Though the Church fathers embraced the full deity of all three Persons, God the Father was understood to be the *source* of deity for the Son and the Spirit, having primacy over the other two. Thus they spoke of the monarchy of the Father.

This view is not without merit, and to dismiss it altogether would be misguided. Viewing the "monarchy" in these terms establishes ample basis for affirming the necessity of executive leadership, which we will talk about in a later chapter. Yet this emphasis led some Church leaders to take the small but consequential step of defining the very essence of the Godhead in *only* these terms. If the Son was subordinate to the Father, as seen in the salvation drama, then He must have been subordinate throughout eternity. And so we come to Arius, a popular presbyter from Alexandria, who in A.D. 318 stated flatly that since the Son is seen in Scripture to be subordinate to the Father, He is, in fact, eternally subordinate and of a different substance (*ousia*).

Of course, this idea threatened the very core of the Gospel. If the Son was not fully deity, then deity did not die on the cross. And if God—in the Person of the Son— did not really die, *then we are not saved.* At this critical juncture in Church history when the very Gospel was hanging in the balance, a bishop named Athanasius led the counterattack, proclaiming that a creature—however noble and perfect—could not accomplish redemption for humankind. To save us, Christ *had* to be fully divine, reasoned Athanasius. To address the controversy, a council was convened at Nicea in A.D. 325. With meticulous care, Church leaders crafted a finely tuned definition of the Trinity: one *ousia* (meaning "being" or "essence"), three *hypostases* (meaning "persons").

Bible students learn early on that the Father, Son and Holy Spirit are co-eternal (they have *always* been God together), co-essential (they are *exactly* the same divine "stuff") and co-equal (one Person is not less divine than the other two). It is this "co-equal" part that we need to understand better if we want to both handle authority wisely and respond to authority with humility and integrity. If you take things too far one way, framing the Godhead in a chain of command in which the Father is the Chairman of the Board, the Son is the Chief Executive Officer and the Spirit is the Chief Operations Officer, I suggest you will find yourself going down the path of our old friend Arius and ultimately compromising truth.

On the other hand, there does seem to be order to the way the Three relate. For example, based on the biblical record we always speak of God as *Father, Son and Spirit*. So how do we reconcile the idea of the Three sharing authority yet the Father having a place of preeminence? This is an issue we want to explore in subsequent chapters.

The Key to Permanent Change

The important idea to see here is that if we are going to be changed fundamentally in our thinking about authority, we must take our cue from God's nature. Otherwise we merely will be attempting to change our behaviors without changing our values. Only when we see how authority is expressed within God's own nature will we be changed at the level of our values, and it is only at this level that we go beyond cosmetic alteration to a permanent transformation.

As followers of Jesus, aligning to authority is not only about fixing our personal world but also about fixing the Church. For we are members of something corporate, something communal—the Body of Christ. This is not just about a peaceful "self" but about a joyous Church. We may not all be in leadership positions (though we all exercise influencing leadership to some degree), but it is vital that we explore the issue of leadership—which we will do in the latter part of the book—because much about this issue of authority is about how leaders handle authority and how we respond to a leader's delegated authority. How authority plays out in the leadership systems of a church is germane to each and every one of our personal releases into greater freedom. A happy church has a lot to do with a happy you and me.

And that is why taking a good, hard look at God is essential. For by looking at how God walks in community and authority within the fellowship of the three Persons, we can better see how the community of the Church is to be structured. And by measuring the Church against this plumb line—that of the Trinity—we may be able to discover more freeing authority structures.

The Triune model of sublime selflessness speaks sweetly and violently to a power-brokering world: sweetly in that we see the wonder of undiluted love, violently in that it stands in militant opposition to any political edifice or church system built on pride. As Leonardo Boff has stated, when the life of the Godhead is allowed to inform and shape society and the Church:

> The domination model is replaced by the communion model: productions by invitation, conquest by participation. The Trinity understood in human terms as a communion of Persons lays the foundation for a society of brothers and sisters, of equals, in which dialogue and consensus are the basic constituents of living together in both the world and the church.[5]

These are timely words for us as believers who should especially be marked by such communal dynamics and relational sensitivities. The healthiest church structures are ones that reflect the ways the Father, Son and Holy Spirit relate to each other—for it is in this reflection that we touch the eternal goodness of the divine nature.

6

How God Models
Authority

In order to become the master, the politician poses as the
servant.

Charles de Gaulle

In the early 1960s a young psychology doctoral candidate by
the name of Stanley Milgram conducted a series of experiments at Yale University to see just how far people would go
in obedience to an authority figure. The memory of World
War II stalked Western civilization. Many high-ranking Nazi
officers, like Adolf Eichmann, were still being indicted for
unspeakable atrocities, and what made these trials so dis-

turbing was that these officers defended themselves by stating that they were just following orders.

Milgram wanted to measure how compliant the average person was when given orders by someone in authority. He especially wanted to see if the average person would comply even if the orders violated his sense of morality. To do this he staged a fake "learning exercise" between two people he labeled "learner" and "teacher." In the exercise the teacher would read word pairs, which the learner was supposed to remember to associate. The learner was strapped to a chair, immobile. Attached to his arms were electrodes connected to a generator controlled by the teacher. The teacher then began reading the first word of each pair, followed by four possible answers. The stern experimenter told the teacher to pull a switch on the generator, which delivered an electric shock to the learner, each time the learner responded incorrectly. These shocks were automatically delivered in increasing intensity up to 450 volts—a lethal level.

What the teacher did not know was that the learner was really an actor, and that he was not really connected to the generator at all. His job was to give wrong answers purposefully, then pretend as if he were receiving the shocks each time the teacher pulled the switch. The alarming result was that most teachers would continue to deliver shocks to their corresponding learners even when the voltage reached dangerous levels. Even when the teacher became extremely uneasy, he would defer to the experimenter—the "authority figure"—who would command him to keep delivering the electric shocks.

The results of this experiment were indeed "shocking": 65 percent of the teachers administered electric shocks up to the full 450 volts, and *no* teacher stopped before reaching 300 volts—which in reality would cause excruciating pain to a person.

Writing in *Harper's Magazine* some years later, Milgram, commenting on the willingness of adults to go to almost any lengths in response to the command of an authority, summarized the implications of this experiment: "Stark authority was pitted against the subjects' strongest moral imperatives against hurting others, and, with the subjects' ears ringing with the screams of the victims, authority won more often than not."[1]

Our tendency to be overly compliant may be the obvious point of this study. But there are two subtexts that are just as important. First, what is underneath most of this compliance is *fear of authority*. The teachers in the experiment were afraid of the consequences their resistance to orders might cause them. These kinds of scenarios, in which authority figures wield illegitimate control, create suspicions in us that *we* are going to be controlled, or even abused.

Second, the authority figure in these experiments was seen as an authority because he possessed the power necessary to compel the subjects to do his will. Authority is mostly seen as the use of power—who has the control. In fact, a common definition of *authority* is "legitimated power in which 'authority' is often one-sided, favoring the ruler."[2] But is that the *right* way to look at authority?

The Difference between Headship and Authority

One of the most important implications we can draw from God's model of authority is to understand the difference between headship, authority and leadership. All too often we treat these as synonymous terms, but there are, in fact, some crucial distinctions to make; for if we confuse them we may find ourselves abusing authority, if we are leaders, or not rightly submitting to authority, if we are followers. In 1 Corinthians 11:3, Paul sketches for us what amounts to a chain of command, as it were: God is the head of Christ, Christ is the head of man and man is the head of woman (the latter relationship dealing specifically with the husband-wife relationship).

If God is the head of Christ, then does that make Christ lesser in divinity? Have we not already seen that in order to maintain the essential truth of the co-equality of the three Persons in the Godhead that authority (the "monarchy") is shared? But then why does Scripture seem to give the Father some preeminence? How do we reconcile what seems to be the priority of the Father and the co-equality of the Three?

This conundrum is deeply felt from business corridors to church foyers. How can authority be shared while still holding to the need for a key leader? This is the dilemma of "the one and the many." How can we be collaborative on the one hand and still allow a leader to command on the other, when "commanding" is genuinely called for? Recently, a friend of mine who serves as a coach to several CEOs told me that many of his clients have grown weary with the "collaborative" approach to management that has dominated business models for the past decade. They contend that, over time, egalitarianism has spawned a culture of entitlement that actually has slowed down the processes of decision making to such a degree that morale has eroded.

I believe the way forward here is to draw a subtle but critical distinction between "authority," "headship" and "leadership." Perhaps one way to carve this is to see that authority is a shared dynamic in which there is mutuality in decision making and "authoring." But in this mutuality, this sharing, the role of headship is crucial in that a head actually *allows* the flow of authority to be shared. Going further, I would suggest that leadership is not so much a role but an action that a head and/or a group undertake. Although for purposes of popular use it is practical to use the terms "head" and "leader" interchangeably, by making this distinction we may be better able to create a culture in which *everyone* can see himself or herself as a "leader" in the sense that everyone, while not a "head" of something, can take the initiative to lead out in something. What we need to better understand is how headship functions.

To say that the Father is the head of Christ does not make Christ lesser. It is not to make the Son inferior. For the Father as "head" means that He is the source of divine life for the Godhead. That is the Father's "place," which is no more important than the Son's or the Spirit's. Headship is thus not about power or position, but "placement." Headship does not exclusively mean "authority over," but "first in place."[3]

What does it mean to be the "head"? First, it means going first—like the headwaters of a river. It means the willingness to take the initiative, to take the risks and go out in front. To be "head" means to exercise leadership, but leadership is not initially about using power; it is the act of going first. Sometimes leadership is a position, but not always; it *is*, however, always an act. It is better to see leadership as an action, not a position. In this way we can encourage *everyone* to be a leader in the sense that Robert Clinton defines it—which is responsibility to influence people toward God's purposes.[4] But not everyone can be "head" at the same time. In better distinguishing between headship and leadership we can avoid confusion and ungodly ambition.

Second, the head "saves." Going first as the "head" means being committed to creating an environment—whether in a company or a marriage—in which everyone is able to rise to his or her potential. In a way, this is what Jesus has done: He has made it possible for us to realize our God-given purpose. This is a part of what it means when we say, "He saved us." And in a sense this is how a head "saves" those under his or her headship. The head of a company, for example, does not need to "lead" all the time, but he or she *does* need to provide "headship" by directing everyone's acts of leadership toward the company's mutually agreed-upon goals and values and creating a climate in which their full potential can be realized.

The head of a team leads the process of coming into unity, ensuring that each member's potential is realized, and gives a sense of context and timing to direction, whether it comes from himself or someone else on the team. The head *manages* the sharing of authority; he is not the sole authority himself.

Does this mean there is never a person with whom the buck stops? Does this mean that a group or a marriage that just cannot come into unity on a given issue is stuck? And does this not then place absolute authority in "the group," so that in reality the one who dissents is really in authority anyway?

This is where the idea of "head" is so helpful. One who confuses authority and headship is one who feels that his directives should be followed automatically, even if those directives are not expressed in the most loving ways. This can lead to resistance among those who—rightly—feel that authority is a more shared relationship between leader and follower. But those who feel this way can inadvertently undermine a leader and court insubmissiveness in their attitudes by thinking that shared authority means shared headship. What they need to catch is the servant role that a head plays *precisely at the point where a group is stalemated.* For if a group's head attempts to lead the process of helping that group come into unity on a given decision, and if that group simply cannot come into unity, and if tabling the decision does more harm to the group than making a decision, there has to be a place where the buck stops so that the group can move forward.

Headship, then, is the last resort of effective decision making. So in this sense authority is vested in the head. The Father is the "head" of the Son, the husband the "head" of his wife, the pastor the "head" of a local congregation. But again, headship does not imply unilateral use of authority but rather ensuring the process of *sharing* authority. Understanding this can protect us from abuses of authority on the one hand and attitudes of rebellion on the other.

How God Handles Authority

So far we have discussed how God's nature shapes our understanding of the structures of authority. But how does God's character speak to us here? Remember, God's *nature* is that which we can never be. And it is His nature that gives us design for our *structures*. His *character* is that which we must be, by the power of the Spirit, and it is this aspect of God that should inform and shape how we handle authority.

Specifically, how does God handle His authority?

I think the best jumping-off place for this question is to consider the two divine *missions* we see in Scripture. As the biblical story unfolds, we see the Father, Son and Holy Spirit engaged primarily in two actions: creation and redemption. God's first act is *creating* the universe. But as we know, our first parents opened the door for sin to enter the world through their rebellion against His authority. So that set in motion the other major activity of God on which the rest of the Bible story is focused, and that is God's action in *redeeming* us. The way He accomplished—and is accomplishing— redemption is first by providing a way back for us, which is centered in the work of the Son; and second by giving us the power to walk that path, which is centered in the work of the Holy Spirit.

Let's take these two words, *creation* and *redemption*, and distill them to two corresponding words that we can apply. We will turn first to the concept of redemption to understand better how God handles authority.

God Models before He Manages

God's acts of redemption converge in the miracle of the incarnation. He became not just a man *but a baby*! Why did God do that? If His intent was to be the sacrifice for the sins of humankind, He could have done that by materializing as a man and then going to the cross. But rescuing us required more. God knew that to feel as we feel, He had to experience the whole lot of human suffering, from rejection to temptation to death. And by walking as we walk, He *modeled* for us His design for life—and this is the essence of the incarnation. God did not just provide a set of principles to live by or a creed to understand. God became flesh and showed us, *modeled* for us, His design for life.

Now He could have just told us what to do, and He would have had a perfect right to do so. He could have managed us by decree. But He didn't just *tell* us what to do; He *showed* us what to do. In a sense, He *modeled* before He *managed*. And this is a key to understanding how God does—and subsequently how we should—handle authority.

God's example of modeling speaks to an even more basic revelation: that God is humble. We think of humility as something that we as creatures are to express, when in fact the humility to which God calls us is central to His own character! God does not command us to do anything that He Himself does not do. The humility God calls us to walk in is that in which He Himself walks. That is why He models before He manages. His willingness to model effervesces from His humility.

The bottom line is that *God expresses authority through humility.* And pictures of His humility are sprinkled liberally throughout the Word. Let's take a closer look at the idea that God models.

Though we see Him modeling His will for us supremely in the incarnation, the humility that compels Him to model His ways for us can be seen at the dawn of Creation as well. God could have spoken everything into existence instantaneously. But He took seven days. Why? I suggest that God wanted to model something for us. The process by which He created was not for Him, but for us. He subjected Himself to limitation, to constraints. He restrained Himself to what was to be humanity's life rhythm, seven days—and in so doing showed us how to live within boundaries. The God who cannot be bounded sets up the workweek; and before He tells Adam to steward creation, He "puts His shift in" to show us how to do it, by voluntarily doing in seven days what He could have done in a nanosecond!

God leads by example—and that is humility. Humility is the wellspring of handling authority, and why we are going to spend an entire chapter on humility later on. The integrity at the very heart of God's character constrained Him to model first and command second. Anytime someone attempts to exercise authority apart from humility, the very authority he grasps slowly entwines him in a lust for power that, over time, will actually rob him of personhood.

God shows the way before He commands us to follow. He saw to it that each day was good before going on to the next day. In this way God was modeling for us the best life-sustaining process. Each day, each step, was intended to demonstrate a unique part of that process. That is, God pushed the pause button at each phase and allowed Himself to sense its goodness, and in so doing helped us identify and appreciate the facets of Creation. Unless God had paused long enough to help us see the benefits of each stage of Creation, we would not have been able to orient ourselves to that rhythm. God's commitment to model work for us was His way of teaching us value in the world He was giving us.

For example, light and darkness had to be separated and it had to be *seen* as that which had been separated. It was not enough for God to do it—we needed to see it. Because God did this, He was able to show humankind what time is all about. Because God modeled something for us and allowed Himself to be limited by the stages of Creation, man was able to understand the concept of time. And of course we know that understanding the concept of time is important if we are to be able to manage our lives well.

So in the Creation story we see God modeling a willingness to work within boundaries.

God Empowers Rather Than Controls

Now let's look at the other word pertaining to God's divine mission, *creation*, and the corresponding word that will help us understand another aspect of how God handles authority—which will, in turn, help us know how to handle authority. At Creation, God *blessed*. God blessed the man and the woman and said, "Be fruitful and multiply; fill the earth and subdue it" (Genesis 1:28, NKJV). The first way we saw God handle authority was by *modeling*. Here we see another key way God handles authority, and that is by *blessing*.

To bless conveys the idea of enduing someone with power for success and prosperity. *God empowers rather than controls*. Make no mistake, He *is* in control, but His method of control is empowerment and protection. That is, He desires to accomplish His will by empowering us, and He will exert constraints only if His creation—and His plan for you—is in jeopardy, as it was in the time of the Great Flood.

God did not seek to use His creation for some other means. Humanity was an end, not a means. Because God is unselfish love, we must conclude that the reason God made humankind was not so more creatures would give Him more glory. God simply gave Himself. So valuable are we to Him that He wants us to adore that which is of the highest worth. His command to worship Him does not spring from anything that would hint of ego, but rather is consistent with the nature of His love. As Shug says to Celie in Alice Walker's novel *The Color Purple*, "When God tells us to focus on Him, He ain't bein' selfish. He jes wanna share a good thing!"

God does not use people as resources for some ulterior goal. To "bless" is to say, "I will live for your success." God does this by creating the resources necessary to allow the man and the woman to fulfill their purposes (see Genesis 1:28–30).

To handle authority well, we need to follow God's example. We need to not only model before managing but also pursue a culture that blesses rather than uses. Many of us are reserved about yielding to somebody's authority because we are afraid we will be used for some other agenda. That is why a climate of blessing should be created in a group of people before goals are pursued. If we pursue other goals and agendas before creating a culture of blessing, we invite a controlling atmosphere.

Humility Legitimates True Authority

There are many examples of God's humility in the Scriptures, the most disarming expressed through Jesus: the servant's towel, the Lamb silent in the face of hostility, the cookout at Galilee after He had risen, the chat with a despised woman at a well. Images of divine humility gild the Gospel story in a dignity found no other place.

But one of the most striking images, I think, is the scene in John 20 in which Jesus first revealed Himself after He rose from the dead. It was not to the pious or the politicos. Nor was it to the masses who had hailed Him earlier with their hosannas. Nor even to His closest companions with whom He had shared life and ministry for over three years.

Jesus showed Himself first to a woman with a past. A woman of questionable reputation. A woman cast off by many, but whose crimson garments had been washed whiter than snow!

And to this woman He revealed Himself, not as the Great Lord of Wonder but as . . . a gardener. At least that is who she thought He was. But the very fact that she thought Him a gardener shows how plain and simple was the manner in which He came to her, how much she thought He was one like her.

And that is the point!

The Lord enters her world at that moment unobtrusively, with the bearing of a common workman. Yet by doing so He shows His delight in identifying with simple, needy humanity! The risen Lord—so close to the toils and difficulties of life that He is mistaken for an ordinary gardener.

Jesus, here, affirms the *glory of the ordinary*. He knew that not everyone would be a rock star, a senator or a business titan.

We would rather fantasize about improbable futures. For many of us, ours is a tabloid world where we can dream of being rich and famous—and important. The mundane has become odious to us. There is little sizzle to a life of carpooling and conflict solving. Yet in this encounter the "glorious Gardener" is speaking precisely to all whose life just seems so "discard-able." The ordinary and overlooked are the most significant to Him!

And what were His first words to this woman? Amazingly, they were not expressed as command, declaration or even simple statement. His first words were in the form of a *question*! And even then, the question centered on *her*, not on *Him*!

"Why are you weeping?" (verse 13, NKJV).

If anyone had the right to announce His preeminence, His "status," it was Jesus. If anyone had the right to be worshiped at that moment, it was Jesus. But instead He asks, "Why are you weeping?" No need to assert His ascendancy here.

The question is so very centered on Mary. "Why are *you* weeping?" It is almost as if the Lord means for her, and us, to see this question as *His most important interest*—the great question to which His resurrection power is the ultimate answer. It is as if He is saying, "Let me show you right from the get-go not only the *power* of My resurrection but the *priority* of My heart! I will meet you at your point of weeping—now and always!"

This is Christ at His core: humility clothed with compassion.

The Greek word for *compassion* is related to a Hebrew word that means "womb of God." God's tender compassion is not the emotion of a beneficent king who has to display such nobility in order to underscore his dignity. No, God's compassion is the expression of the deep birth pangs He feels for broken people.

That glorified Savior in the garden was God in labor— pursuing one overlooked outcast! And this, I think, is the essence of the resurrected Jesus.

In the Ukraine there was a well-known Hasidic rabbi, Levi Yitzhak, who told a story of two Polish peasants—Ivan and Peter—both tipsy in a tavern, each protesting to the other how he loved the other better. Finally, Ivan said to Peter, "Peter, tell me, what hurts me?"

Peter, in slurred speech, asked, "How do I know what hurts you?"

Ivan swiftly replied, "If you don't know what hurts me, how can you say you love me?"

That is what Jesus was trying to say in this garden: *He knows what hurts you, and what hurts you is His priority.*

Our Lord's example of humility defines genuine authority. And it is to this central of all graces—humility—that we now turn.

7

Bridled by the Spirit (Humility on the Inside)

I saw all the devil's traps set upon the earth. I groaned and said, "Who can pass through them?" And I heard a voice saying: "Humility."

St. Anthony

Corrie ten Boom, who survived the horrors of a Nazi concentration camp to become God's globetrotting messenger of love and forgiveness, used to tell an incisive parable about a woodpecker that captures the audacity of pride. This handsome woodpecker spent much of his time pecking away at tall trees in the forest. Day after day, one could hear the rat-a-tat-tat of the little bird. One day the woodpecker took on an exceptionally tall redwood. The enormity of the tree was matched only by the woodpecker's ferocious determination. He perched himself high upon the redwood's trunk and began pecking away—oblivious to the gusts of wind signaling an approaching thunderstorm.

Before long the storm was swirling around the woodpecker. But no matter; he was determined to finish his job. Then all at once a bolt of lightning struck the giant tree, sending it crashing to the ground—just at the precioo moment the woodpecker gave it a mighty peck.

Startled, the bird fluttered away to a safe distance. But he quickly surveyed what had just happened and saw that the great tree had fallen. The woodpecker swelled with pride. *My*, he said to himself, *what power there is in my beak!*

The bird's sentiments are not too removed from the secret thoughts of our own hearts. For we often strive hard to succeed, scratching our way to some pinnacle of achievement; and having done so we think that our personal moxie has gotten us there—forgetting all too easily that *all* we have and *all* we are flow from the graciousness of God. Only when we finally "let go and let God" will we discover the defrauding masquerade of pride and the curative of humility, that—in the words of Henri Frederic Amiel—"True humility is contentment."

Humility is being under the control of the Holy Spirit. As in dressage, in which a horse that has been broken responds in poetic choreography to the control of its rider, so we are to be "broken" by the Spirit, that we may respond with quick grace to His leading.

Measuring Brokenness

Where we lack humility is often difficult to detect because pride is so difficult to see. Here are some questions to ask ourselves that may help us measure our brokenness.

What would you do if . . .

- You hear something negative about another person or ministry that you secretly distrust?
- Your gifts and talents are continuously overlooked in a group you are part of?
- You are given a chance to promote a rival ministry in an opportunity you really wanted?
- You sense tension in a relationship but do not know why it is there?
- Someone younger than you—less talented, less experienced and less mature—is placed over you in a leadership position (especially if that person thinks he is more talented and mature than he really is)?
- You are part of a problem-solving group dealing with an issue that is in your primary area of expertise, but you are not chairing the group?
- Someone in authority corrects you?
- Someone under your authority corrects you?
- You begin to have questions about the direction an organization or the church in which you are involved is taking?
- Someone criticizes your work after you put an enormous amount of effort into it?
- Someone is brought into your organization who obviously has more talent in your area than you do?
- You are in leadership and you are challenged by some of your followers?
- You find yourself rejected or criticized and you sense an acute need for affirmation?

- You know you have said or done something that has offended another person?
- You are asked to do something you are not gifted to do and have no desire to do?
- Someone greatly offends you but later comes to you asking for forgiveness—and you know that to forgive her would mean that she would not suffer any consequences for the hurt she brought you?
- Your child does something that really embarrasses you in front of those you most want to impress?
- Your staff member/employee does something that embarrasses you or severely handicaps your ability to accomplish your goals?
- You are angrily rebuked for reasons you cannot understand?
- Someone questions your judgment?
- A close associate who is under your leadership finds himself attracted to another ministry or company?
- Someone teaches something you disagree with?

Marks of Brokenness

Humility goes by many words: brokenness, meekness, gentleness. But spiritual brokenness has little to do with the idea of being grieved, sorrowful or down in the dumps. Meekness has nothing to with weakness. In the Greek of the New Testament, the word *meek* means "mild, gentle, humble"—it points to the individual who does not seek control. That is the essence of it. The "meek" person is one who does not try to control anything but himself. The following definition of *brokenness* hits the bull's-eye: "the person who strives to control nothing—and no one—but himself." And as we have already seen, authority is measured by the degree to which we control ourselves (see Proverbs 16:32). Ironically, we control ourselves by letting go of ourselves and yielding to the Holy Spirit.

Numbers 12:3 reports that Moses was more meek, or humble, than anyone else on the face of the earth. Psalm 25:9 says, "The meek will he guide in judgment: and the meek will he teach his way" (KJV). Jesus stated, "Blessed are the meek, for they will inherit the earth" (Matthew 5:5). It has been said that a good definition of *meekness* is "controlled strength." As good as that is, I do not think that definition goes far enough. For it implies that the act of controlling—self-control—originates in our will alone. But the spiritual fruit of self-control has to do with a control of the self that comes by way of tying it to a larger authority. In other words, *self-control is a synonym for dependence.*

The broken individual is the individual who has let go of his life. We find this in Moses, who did not defend himself when accused (see Numbers 16); we find this in David, who did not react to criticism nor hold on to his authority (see 2 Samuel 16:5–14). We certainly see its most pristine expression in the incarnation of Christ. "Can we see the divine humility in the way that Word of God was spoken? Can we see the even greater humility when the Word of God was spoken in the middle of the night through the splayed legs of a teenage girl in the barnyard stench of a stable, where divine eloquence was reduced to the whimper of a child?"[1]

God values spiritual brokenness above every other attitude. What are some of the marks of a spiritually broken person?

He is easily correctable.

In fact, the broken person actively seeks correction (see Proverbs 3:11–12; 9:8). He does not stiffen when reproved, is not quick to jump to his defense. The manner of his voice, his body language, his sweetness of spirit, all express an appetite for adjustment. The Lord, through Jeremiah, makes a startling pronouncement: "In vain I have struck down your sons, you did not accept correction: your sword devoured your prophets like a destructive lion" (Jeremiah 2:30, JB). Refusing correction makes us devourers of others. The text here is speaking of the messengers of God they destroyed, but the application is universal. A lack of "teachability" makes us proud and defensive, prone to use and manipulate people to our advantage. Those who "devour" are themselves ultimately "devoured."

He strives for excellence in the unseen things.

We are familiar with the concept that character is revealed by how we act privately, when nobody sees us. What I am in my private moments, what I think in my innermost thoughts, how I act in the company of those with whom I feel totally secure—this is when the "real me" surfaces. Again, better is "he who rules his spirit" than "he who captures a city" (Proverbs 16:32, NASB). How we think of others in the privacy of our own minds, how we respond to irritation when no one is looking—these things are not only the test of character but the harbinger of public authority.

What we are able to handle publicly is determined by the habits we cultivate privately. Why? Because in the private areas of our lives we have no agenda. It is relatively easy to be gracious and patient when someone is looking over our shoulder or when we are secretly trying to impress a superior. But what we are often doing in these cases is trying to control how others perceive us. When we pursue godliness in the private moment, there is nothing to control. By focusing on the private disciplines of prayer and fasting and generosity, we are "leaning into" genuine humility.

He perceives ministry as an overflow of relationship.

This is an important characteristic to consider. Often we approach ministry like we would approach our career—always looking for relationships and circumstances we can broker to our advantage, always with an eye to climbing ladders of opportunity. I did a music project some time ago. Having produced the project, I proceeded to assign the distribution rights to a certain record company. We had been negotiating the contract for a few months, and I was about a week from actually signing the contract, when a larger, more prominent record company heard my project and tendered an offer. I knew that if I went with the larger company I would sell vastly more units. But I also knew that I had key relationships in this other, smaller company and had already "walked down the aisle" with these people.

The determining factor for me in my decision was relationship. Where had God sown me? Where were my relationships already flowing? I had very little relationship with the larger company, although that partnership would have been a better opportunity. I considered where my primary relationships were and realized that I needed to stay the course. I was to be driven not by opportunity but by the integrity that seeks to honor relationships.

He actively seeks to promote others' ministries.

This can be a tough one. When I first began my traveling ministry, I was asked to speak at a large youth camp in Ohio. I had a fair read on my gifts and strengths and knew that I was not a bad speaker. After all, I had been a youth pastor for a decade. But I was not a real bell-ringer either. The first night of the camp was a pretty mediocre showing on my part. The next day I was feeling unsettled and a little insecure. Then I received a call in my room from one of the largest churches in the nation. They wanted me to come and do a youth conference. I felt a rush of excitement race through me—*I was becoming a known quantity!* I asked them when, they gave me the dates, I looked at my calendar and my heart sank. I was already booked at another church the weekend they wanted me—a church that was, by comparison, small and insignificant.

The first test was a test of integrity: Would I cancel the little engagement in order to book the big one? I knew I could not do that and live with myself, so that was not a hard test to pass. I told them that I could not accept their invitation at that time.

As I was finishing up the conversation, the Lord whispered in my heart that I was to tell them of another person who could fill that date for them. I frowned. The problem, you see, was that this particular person was better than me at everything. He could preach, teach, lead worship, tell jokes and hold an audience better than me. My heart sank even further. *Lord, if I tell them about this guy and they have him come, they'll never want me since this guy's so much better.* Nevertheless, the Lord pressed me to promote this brother's ministry. So, feeling like a man going to the guillotine, I referred them to this other speaker. They thanked me, and I hung up—feeling pretty miserable.

But that night an extraordinary thing happened. As I finished preaching to those four hundred young people, a strong, muscular high schooler fell flat on his back. Nobody had touched him. There was nothing emotionally charged in the service that would have elicited that kind of response. At first I thought he had fainted or was having a seizure, so I stepped off the platform to get someone to call an ambulance. About that time one of his friends started crying, saying that God was touching the boy's body. Apparently he was a football player and had sustained an injury, and God was completely healing him. It was one of those spontaneous, sovereign sorts of things that cannot be explained except in terms of God's intervention. I knew it was not psychologically induced, since I had not struck any significant chord that night with the audience. No "mood music" was being played. God just decided to touch that guy.

Well, the rest of the evening was amazing. Young people came to Christ in large numbers; others were touched in extraordinary ways. In short, we experienced a divine visitation that evening that lasted throughout the rest of the camp. To this day, many who were there that week speak of the camp as a defining moment in their lives.

That night, as I lay upon my bed, the Lord impressed upon me a life principle: If I would be careful to promote other people's ministries, He Himself would promote mine.

He does not have a possessive attitude toward his gifts.

As I was just beginning my trek into full-time Christian service years ago, I remember praying one night and God asked me if I would be willing to give my ministry role to another. Would I be willing to step down and allow someone else to have the role that I was very much enjoying? It was a struggle for me, but I finally said yes to the Lord. He did not actually ask me to step down at that point; I have tried, however, to hold my leadership loosely ever since. Not everyone, perhaps, may be asked to do that. But if the Lord ever requires it, it is only that He might be able to expand our borders. When the herdsmen of Abraham and Lot quarreled, it was Abraham who allowed Lot to have first pick of the land—Abraham was quite willing to take what was left over. Lot chose Sodom. And Abraham became the father of billions!

He has relinquished his need for affirmation to the Lord.

He is free from having to establish his self-worth. We must be wary of the incessant itch for affirmation; such an obsession exposes a lack of trust in the Lord. If we are constantly looking for a pat on the back or an encouraging word, we actually may be looking more to people to fulfill needs than God. This invariably sets up a cycle: The more we go to people to meet those psychological needs, the deeper those needs seem to become. The affirmation that comes from people alone does not really stick to our spiritual ribs. If their encouragement is a prompt from God, and they are the instrument through whom *God* is fulfilling our need, that is heavenly manna indeed (see Hebrews 3:13). When *we* seek encouragement from people without allowing the Lord to dispense it through them in His perfect time, we are like little children blowing bubbles—finding that as soon as we put our finger to them they vanish. So it is with "seeking encouragement" rather than seeking God.

He is not defensive, nor does he seek to vindicate or justify himself.

Spiritual brokenness is possessing the spirit of the Lamb who "opened not His mouth" (Isaiah 53:7, NKJV). It is to rest in the truth that *the Lord* will vindicate us when we are wronged or someone smudges our reputation (see Isaiah 54:17). Years ago, when I was first traveling as an itinerant preacher, my reputation took a hit, which, in retrospect, turned out to be pretty comical. I was living in California at the time and was scheduled to minister on the East Coast. I found out just weeks before going on the trip that a number of churches had blackballed my ministry. They had heard I had been "defrocked" because of some supposed immoral conduct.

When I was told that, I just laughed, though it meant my reputation was briefly sullied. It seems that there was another minister from California with the same name who had been dismissed from his denomination because of his indiscretions. A few pastors had jumped to conclusions and assumed that I was that man. But I felt no need to vindicate or defend myself—I knew that vindication comes from the Lord. Soon the whole matter cleared up and my reputation was restored. The truly broken person will not seek to defend himself when ridiculed or criticized. He does not seek to control his reputation but rather allows the Lord to be his defense.

He does not fight seasons of obscurity.

This does not mean that we will be no-names all our lives. Nor does it mean that ambition is neutered. It just means that we have no problem being unknown—that the itch for recognition, the need to be seen, has been thoroughly purged from our spiritual systems, that we are ambitious for *God's* agenda, not ours.

We are not to seek anonymity any more than we are to seek prestige. True north for our moral compass is that which most glorifies God—whether by being unknown or well known. A. W. Tozer writes, "It is altogether unlikely that we know who our greatest men are . . . for the holy man is also the humble man and the humble man *will not advertise himself nor allow others to do it for him*."[2]

The one bridled by the Spirit looks for the path of least personal interest. In other words, he prefers others to himself. This does not mean that a broken person mirrors Victor Hugo's Hunchback: the butt of ridicule, the one always used for others' advantage. Sometimes the path of least personal interest means the bold willingness to confront someone even if our personal agenda is thwarted or the work we have built comes apart.

The broken person thinks of himself last, and this both enables him to look to others' benefit and frees him from having to preserve his own. He neither kowtows to another for the sake of saving his own skin, nor is he always inclined to look for political advantage, for ways he can become king of the mountain. This is a supreme mark of "dying to self." St. John of the Cross once wrote, "I live when I can no longer die." In other words, life begins when all that can be dead in us *is*!

He is not driven by opportunity.

I was tested on this one early on in my itinerate ministry. I had been traveling for a couple of years and God was steadily building my reputation around the country. About two years into this journey the Lord asked me to stop traveling for three months and take no opportunities if they came. I endeavored to be obedient to that. But a month into this season I received a call from a very prestigious organization asking me to preach at a major conference they were sponsoring. I knew I was going to have to turn it down, based on what God had required me to do, but I died a hundred deaths inside. I knew that by taking this particular engagement my reputation as a sought-after preacher and worship artist would hit a whole new level. Yet I told them no. I knew I had to pass this test of not being driven by opportunity.

That was years ago. That organization did not call me back for a long time. In the meantime, however, other opportunities opened up that were much more substantial than that one ever was. If we pass this test, God will show Himself faithful.

He is not afraid to admit he is wrong and is quick to ask for forgiveness.

One of my mentors, Joy Dawson, once observed that a person can always tell how broken he is by how long it takes him to ask for forgiveness from one he has offended. If a person has knowingly offended another and it takes an hour or two to humble himself and go ask for the other's forgiveness, that person is fairly unbroken. Should it be a day that transpires before asking for forgiveness, that person is *very* unbroken.

Conclusion

My wife, Nancy, who is something of a horse authority, had this insight: "A wild and free horse may make a romantic image . . . but it is useless. A dressage horse is one *with* the rider. It usually does not strain against the bit or resist being trained. If it does strain against the bit when being trained, it develops something called 'proud neck'—a malady that reduces the flexibility of the neck due to repeated strains against the bit."

These are wise words for us all, words that are echoed in Proverbs 29:1: "A man who remains stiff-necked after many rebukes will suddenly be destroyed—without remedy."

8

Bucking Our Boundaries

I have as much authority as the Pope;
I just don't have as many people who believe it.

George Carlin

Over the years, I have had the privilege of leading several
ministry teams with diverse agendas in a variety of settings.
Some have been short-term assignments, others longer term.
In these team-leading settings I would, from time to time,
encounter attitudes in individuals that seemed to convey
resistance either to my leadership or toward the consensus
of the team. I do not mean "resistance" in the sense of honest
questioning, but subtle expressions of annoyance—a stiffen-
ing to the idea of compromise, a posture of unyieldedness,
a subconscious oversensitivity about being rejected.

If you have functioned as a leader, you probably can recall times in which you have felt someone resisting your leadership. It may not be something that is said. The resistance is often something that registers in a person's tone of voice or body language. Sometimes it is registered in a team member who just withdraws; you can almost see it in his or her eyes. Psychologists refer to this as being "passive-aggressive," which is a primary method of manipulating others.

I remember processing with one team what this feels like. We tried to come up with imagery that helped us put words and pictures to the subtle, sometimes unspoken, kinds of attitudes that team members can display toward a team leader without even realizing it. One such image was of a cat that arches its back when it is either afraid or displeased about something. So when one of us would stiffen in resistance to authority and leadership, another team member would say, "You're arching your back."

Many times that "arch" was rooted in a complex of emotions. Rarely is it a case of simple rebellion. Such a reaction is often an expression of fear. It may be prompted by a leader saying or doing something that brings to mind hurtful memories. Or it can be based in the threat that the ones who have control have the power to keep us from realizing our hopes and dreams. Leaders should always be aware of the complexity of people's reactions and respond with great patience. This is one reason why Paul cautioned Timothy that when he corrected, rebuked and encouraged that he do so "with great patience and careful instruction" (2 Timothy 4:2).

Still, an "arch" is an "arch," and we need to recognize this response as an indicator that we may have trouble accepting boundaries—which, in turn, may reveal that we have an authority problem. Our view of authority is indeed defined by our attitude toward boundaries, and when we buck our boundaries we are displaying the exact opposite of spiritual brokenness. So let's look at some boundary markers and assess our readiness to align to them. While this list is by no means exhaustive, it will give us at least some sense of how at ease we are with the very concept of boundaries.

Choosing Friends

There is a boundary in the way we are to pick our friends. Proverbs 13:20 says, "He who walks with the wise grows wise, but a companion of fools suffers harm." Picking friends on the basis of their character and not on our emotional preference is a boundary. By allowing the issue of character to determine our closest friends, we are accepting limits to our "wants." We are saying that a person who makes us feel good but whose life is marked by foolishness cannot become a close friend.

We are also saying that we will intentionally pursue those who can better us and provoke us to be more than we are. This, too, is a boundary. Someone who has a healthy, constructive attitude toward authority is someone who is not afraid to be taught by another, even by a peer. Do we have a desire, as Proverbs 27:17 puts it, to be "sharpened" by another? Or do our insecurities keep us from being vulnerable enough to learn?

Sometimes we choose our friends based on what we want, not necessarily on what we need. If, because of our inferiority, we resist vulnerability and do not want to have our weak places exposed, then we may actually be showing that we have an unteachable attitude. This "unteachability" translates to our relationships with people in authority. We can find ourselves envious of their expertise and, again, because of our own insecurities, "arch our back." By choosing wise friends, we are saying to our insecurities that they will not rule us.

Chasing Rainbows

Someone who bucks boundaries is one who chases fantasies. Proverbs 12:11 describes this person: "He who works his land will have abundant food, but he who chases fantasies lacks judgment." Have you ever been around a person who always seems to dream but can never bring those dreams to reality? Sometimes such "dreamers" never see those dreams translated into reachable goals because they have never learned boundaries. A true dream is one that blends our history, our skills and our desires together to form a realistic vision. A fantasy is an escape from the reality of who we are. We either do not like who we are or do not like the circumstances in which we find ourselves. So we fantasize about someone we would like to be or some grand scheme we would like to pursue.

This kind of fantasizing shows an unwillingness to bend to the boundaries of my life history: my "skill set," my heritage, my experiences, others' input. Now it is admirable for a person to reach the limits of his or her potential. And often our experiences can be severely limiting. For example, we applaud rightly the student who, though handicapped by socio-economic hardships, breaks through those barriers to excel in education. But in this case the individual's confining environment was more than offset by his or her innate skills and aptitudes. True dreams tap a person's potential.

But then there are those *American Idol* contestants who insist they have singing talent, when in fact the voice fairy has not graced them by a long shot. For them it is not about pursuing a dream; it is about a puffed-up, unrealistic image of who they are—an image sketched in their minds, no doubt, while they were singing in the shower or fawned over by a friend. Chasing fantasies! Fantasy refuses to accept the boundary of who we are innately. For example, I was never built like a football player, so for me to fantasize about a professional career on the gridiron is foolish.

People who chase get-rich schemes when they can't (or won't) balance their checkbooks, or who dream of a life on Broadway when they can't carry a tune in a bucket, are people who cannot accept the boundaries of their "life mold." This is especially acute for us as Christians, who feel that God made us for a purpose. To fantasize is to wish we were designed differently. To wish we were different is not only an accusation against God, but it also keeps us from genuine fulfillment.

If God made you as you are for a *purpose*, then to resist your design is to resist your own satisfaction. You and I will never be satisfied being somebody else or having someone else's opportunities. For they will not help us accomplish *our own* purpose—and if God made you the way you are, *then He also made you to be happy only by being who you are.* And at the end of the day, gracing the cover of *People* magazine, or receiving the plaudits of some highbrow academy, or landing the top spot at a company will not satisfy you if these achievements are not part of your divine design.

If our dreams do not match our design, not only will we lead frustrated lives, but we will always struggle with authority figures. Inferiority that breeds fantasy leads to futility. Accepting ourselves actually shows a willingness to bend to boundaries.

The Unruly Member

Another sign of a "boundary bucker" is an uncontrolled tongue. Psalm 106 captures the story of that first generation of Israelites delivered from Egypt, who wasted away in the desert because they could not keep from complaining. Controlling what we say is a very important boundary in our lives. Sometimes we think that if we *feel* it we have to *say* it. But that is a lie. Sometimes we may feel the impulse to say something negative or destructive, but at that point we must curb our desire to vent. Some psychologists may tell us that "keeping it in" is not a good thing, but the Scriptures tell us otherwise. James tells us that although the tongue is "a little member," it is "an unruly evil, full of deadly poison" (James 3:5, 8, NKJV).

It is true that what we say is but a reflection of what is already in our hearts, but I submit that it is equally true that by controlling our tongue we can actually reshape our hearts. If life is in the tongue (see Proverbs 15:4), then speaking words of blessing and not words of complaint or criticism actually sows life in our own hearts. So our willingness to control our tongue shows our willingness to accept a boundary. We will not allow ourselves just to express whatever we want to express.

This is especially pertinent in our culture, where our right to express our opinions is often held as a sacrosanct entitlement. In his book *Love Covers*, Paul Billheimer says:

Pride of opinion in non-essentials transcends love; and that is not only sin, it is the worst form of sin—it is idolatry. We set up our opinions as little icons and demand that all others bow down and worship them by agreeing with us. Those who do not we separate from. . . . This may be the essence of carnal pride.[1]

To hold our tongues is to harness ourselves to others. By accepting this boundary we actually put ourselves in a position in which one of our deepest needs can be met: the need to experience *community*. The tongue under control actually creates a safe environment for those around us, which in turn engenders an ease with which they can be honest and genuine with us—which ironically leads to more open and satisfying relationships! Unbridled "openness" may sound all communal and wonderful, but in fact it merely reveals an immaturity that polarizes people in the end.

Harnessing this unruly member does not mean just measuring our words. It also means using our words to build up other people. In fact, one of the ways we exercise authority is to rejoice in another. The reason why this is an important measure of authority is that it shows a heart that understands boundaries. To rejoice at someone else's success is to recognize God's right to draw boundary lines for all of us. If we do not cultivate this attitude, we will soon find ourselves losing authority, which means losing the ability to be self-controlled and losing the privilege of influencing others.

Gotta Have It, Gotta Keep It

Ironically, one of the signs of resistance to boundaries is an attitude of possessiveness and control. And this can come out in all kinds of ways. As a kid—and the firstborn grandson on my father's side—I used to look forward to going to my grandparents' house. I knew that a trip to their house meant treats and freedoms I did not enjoy at my house. Christmas at "Mamoo's" house was especially enjoyable. But as I grew older, I noticed that Christmas was often a stressful affair for her. She seemed so worried about having a good Christmas that she would start planning for it in the summer. It was her way of staying in control of the holiday.

Worry is often a symptom of a controlling attitude. Being possessive, toward relationships or our careers, for example, seems to foment anxiety.

A key test of how possessive we are is in our attitude toward money. How generous are we? Do we fret over not having enough? Do we grimace when someone mentions tithing?

Stinginess reflects a boundary problem. For to be generous means that I am letting go of some of what I think I need to feel secure. When I am generous toward someone or some ministry, it means I am committing myself to them in some way. Likewise, a reluctance to be generous shows an unwillingness to be connected to and dependent on others. You might ask, "How is this a boundary issue? It seems that by holding on to my money I am *setting* a boundary in my life." But actually it may show that we are unwilling to accept the obligations of community and commitment. A lack of generosity shows that we want to be in control, an attitude says, "I am entitled to control the money I earn."

113

This is why the issue of tithing can be a touchy one. Malachi 3:8–10 has some pretty potent things to say about tithing, stating that to withhold the tithe is to rob God. R. T. Kendall, in his book *Tithing: Discover the Freedom of Biblical Giving*, quotes O. S. Hawkins, who cut to the chase on this issue: "The principle hindrance to the advancement of the kingdom of God is greed. It is the chief obstacle to heaven-sent revival. When the back of greed is broken, the human spirit soars."[2]

We can debate till the cows come home about whether tithing is obligatory in the New Testament or only in the Old Testament, and about the ramifications of being under grace rather than under law. The bottom line is how our heart responds when the word *tithing* is mentioned. If we "arch our back," we have a control problem.

The Marriage Partnership

The issue of boundaries is critical when it comes to one of the most important relationships, the relationship between husband and wife. I will devote an entire chapter to this subject as we take a closer look at the marital relationship through the lens of Ephesians 5:21–33. For now, ask yourself—if you are married—some questions. How do you, as a husband, accept the boundary of sacrificing yourself—your wants, your ambitions—for the sake of your wife, as Jesus did for the Church? How do you, as a wife, express proper submission to your husband and let him lead?

Where does "mutual submission" come in? If you have done all you can as a couple to come into unity on an issue—and a decision has to be made—should the husband require that his wife "submit" to his headship? Should the wife require that her husband "sacrifice" his preferences in the name of Christlike love? Should you wait until you *are* in unity, expressing submission one to another?

All these postures can be biblically justified, and we will try to discern some guidelines later on. The key question here is this: Does just the *discussion* of these boundaries make us prickly? Or do we find ourselves praying, *Whatever You require, Lord, I want to be pleasing to You in the way I respond toward my spouse?*

The IRS Measure

> Year after year, as Tax Day nears,
> One can hear the subtle jeers of
> Many cheerless, angry folk
> Who think the government one big joke!

Are we in this cadre of discontented citizens who crack a cynical line or two about how unscrupulous our government is? Our attitude toward civil authority is a clear indicator of whether we have a boundaries problem. Romans 13:1–7 specifies what our responses toward government should be. In our very "independent" America we sometimes forget that God is sovereign over nations and cities. He has put in place—or at least allowed—those in authority in governmental spheres. We may not always understand His larger purposes as to why He puts certain governments in place and not others, but we know He is sovereign over them. In any case, our response to government must be one of obedience (insofar as that what is required does not violate the higher laws of God) and respect.

We have become, in many respects, a brash, uncivil culture. And this incivility has its roots, I believe, in the disrespect we often express in this country toward our governmental leaders. Yes, we should carefully guard our privileges of free speech and the right to dissent. But these freedoms do not entitle us to be mean-spirited. The rudeness we see on the roads, for example, may be rooted in our culture of disrespect for authority in general. What often passes for guarding our deeply held value of personal independence may really be just our insistence that we be entitled to unlimited expression.

Questioning authority is quite different than *disrespecting* authority, and I am afraid that because we have all too easily confused the two—and fostered a climate of disrespect—we have created a calloused society.

The Ultimate Boundary: The Word of God

There is a final boundary issue demanding our focus: our attitude toward the Word. This is one of the most important indicators of whether we are rightly aligned to authority.

I believe we as a Church are, and have been, in crisis because of the way we have minimized the authority of Scripture. This crisis is felt in different ways, and one of those is in the way some allow spiritual experience to determine doctrine. Because we have not understood the authority of Scripture, we have confused spirituality with genuine holiness and encountering God's presence. Many people feel like they are encountering God's presence even when their lives are unrighteous. For example, many homosexuals sincerely feel they can love Christ and experience heartfelt worship and yet maintain a gay lifestyle. But that is not really much different than people who claim they experience the presence of God but whose lives are full of criticism, gossip or greed.

What this shows is a deep confusion between the soul and the spirit—a subject that requires much more exploration than we can give here. Suffice it to say that people who submit to the authority of the Scriptures generally have a greater sense of discernment about things. They can, because of their deep passion for the Scriptures, rightly discern between the soul and the spirit (see Hebrews 4:12). So much is genuinely experienced in the soul, but if it does not line up with biblical authority, then we are set up for deception.

9

Sanded to Fit (Authority and Community)

There are two things over which you have complete dominion, authority and control: your mind and your mouth.

African proverb

An ancient story about a desert father by the name of Abba Anub offers a portrait of genuine humility. Seven young disciples came to him, asking him to establish with them a monastic community. By now Anub was old, but he listened to their request. He then led them to an ancient temple and told them, "Let us live in separate quarters in this temple for seven days, not seeing each other until the week is out."

In the temple stood a stone statue. At dawn every day the old father rose and pelted the statue with stones. In the evening he would come back to that same statue, saying, "Forgive me." The young disciples saw him do this day after day, night after night. It puzzled them. Finally, after seven days they met again, and one of the young upstarts reproved Abbot. "I saw you, Father, throwing stones at the face of the statue, and later doing penance to that statue. A true Christian would not have done so."

To that the old man responded, "For your sakes I did it. When you saw me throwing stones at the statue's face, did it speak? Was it angry?"

"No," they replied.

The old man said again, "When I did penance before the statue, was it troubled in heart? Did it say, 'I do not forgive you'?"

Again they responded that it did not.

"Here we are seven brothers. If we want to stay together, we must become like this statue, which is untroubled by the injuries I have done it. And if you will not become like this statue? See there are four doors to this temple, and each of us may go in the direction he chooses."

Needless to say, the other brothers saw the old man's point and knew that he was calling them to a humility of heart that responds in patience when attacked and is quick to forgive when wronged. They remained together in community for the rest of their lives.[1]

The young men came to see that genuine community is built on a humility that values boundaries and is willing to live within them. How does an inner brokenness make us people who can easily fit into the Body of Christ? How does one with a "bridled spirit" relate to his or her church community?

If authority is the key to personal freedom, and personal freedom is my objective, why even bother to ask these questions? It might seem like "fitting into" a community of believers is asking for restrictions rather than release. How does rightly relating to a community bring us into greater freedom?

Most all of us want to belong to something bigger than ourselves. We want to "fit." But like pieces of a jigsaw puzzle, we need to be in touch with our boundaries if we are going to fit easily with other pieces to make a beautiful whole. Valuing and submitting to authority makes us more apt to welcome boundaries and limits that would help us fit with a group. And fitting actually frees us more than not fitting—because the acceptance we feel when we rightly fit frees us to enjoy a sense of personal worth and significance.

When Solomon built his famous temple, it is said that each stone was cut, sanded and polished in the quarry before it was taken to the temple mount. Prior to being transported to the construction site, the stones had already been prepared with such precision that when they were inserted into the temple walls they were fitted together without the sound of a hammer (see 1 Kings 6:7). God does not want to "pound" us into place—He wants to fit us into place.

So what are the marks of one with a bridled spirit who has been sanded to fit?

He identifies with the structure in which God has placed him.

He promotes change by participating from the inside out. If pressed, he will bend toward renewing existing structures as opposed to spearheading revolutions. He is quick to communicate, "I'm a *part* of you, not a *criticizer* of you."

John Wesley was like this. He did not set out to start the Methodist movement. He tried to renew the Anglican Church—it was his lifelong pursuit. He never wanted to found a new denomination. Yet God Himself intervened and birthed what has now become one of the largest Protestant denominations in the world, Methodism. But the important thing to note is that Wesley did not automatically react against the institution of which he was a part, though it needed some changing. He was a humble man and sought the pathway of renewal rather than revolt.

He looks for God's delegated authorities in every situation.

Years ago I had the privilege of being part of the Youth Leadership Committee for Washington for Jesus, a large interdenominational prayer gathering on the National Mall. A friend of mine who bore the responsibility to lead the youth emphasis of the event assembled fifty or so national youth leaders months ahead of time to design the program for a huge concert at RFK Stadium. There were several notables in the conference room that day as we attempted to develop an appropriate plan and structure.

The leader/moderator was doing his best to accommodate everyone's interests, but discussions soon bogged down because there was no clear flow of authority. The meeting began to get a little unwieldy. I sat back after a couple of hours and surveyed the relational landscape. There were seven or eight in the room who obviously were good friends of this particular leader. I spoke up at that point and said that perhaps the best thing to do would be to free the leader to select a steering committee made up of his primary friendships, whom we would all bless and affirm and with whom this leader could process the details of program and structure. It was a timely word of wisdom at a very important moment and relieved a great deal of pressure. Everybody enthusiastically responded to my suggestion. All I had really done was to take Christ's Lordship to its logical conclusions in that situation. Trying to discern the relational realities helped me determine where the lines of authority were flowing in that particular setting.

Loren Cunningham, the founder of Youth With A Mission, sums up this attitude: "The more mature you become, the more authorities you can submit to."

He is eager to blend with the ministries of others.

The broken person, when placed in a team, will first strive to assess the strengths and weaknesses of his fellow team members and then seek to complement them.

I recall being in a conference some time ago where a number of Christians from a variety of denominational backgrounds had gathered. The worship leader that particular evening displayed substantial insensitivity to his audience. He conducted a worship time that clearly leaned to one particular style. As I looked around, I saw many leaders disconnecting from the worship experience. It did not resonate with their particular spiritual history or tradition. The worship leader seemed oblivious to this. Rather than seek to complement the conference, he was intent on leading the worship segment of the gathering in a way that was dominated by his particular preferences.

The broken person is a "team player," because he has learned that promotion comes from the Lord (see Psalm 75:6–7) and he is thus freed from having to assert his uniqueness.

He allows his ministry to be shaped by members of the Body.

The broken person does not seek to convince others of the value of his ministry. In fact, he is careful not to allow himself to have an inflated estimate of his gifts. In his pursuit of accuracy, he has one ear to the Lord, but one eye to the Body of Christ. There are times, of course, when we have a distinct word from God about what we are to do, and nobody else recognizes that. In those seasons we are to stand fast and hold on to the word God has given us, no matter who does or does not see it. But on the other hand we can stubbornly hold on to images of ourselves and our ministries that are inaccurate and out of place. We mentally and emotionally project ourselves into roles we think will garner more approval.

The broken person measures how other Christians respond to him. If a person insists on pursuing roles and responsibilities that other believers do not seem to rise to, he needs to step back and reassess his ministry, emotionally letting it go. Having done so, he very well may discover that God wants him to pursue that ministry even if *no one* understands it. But at least his pursuit will be grounded in obedience to the Lord, his spirit freed from having to prove himself to others.

He is willing to build on another person's ministry.

We often feel like we have to initiate our own ministry in order to truly own it or have identity with it. Yet we find

123

this humility in Jesus: He was perfectly willing to build on John the Baptist's ministry. In fact, He obtained His first disciples from John's band. If anyone had a right to do his own thing, it was the Son of God. But in humility He was quite willing to build on another's ministry.

He avoids cynicism.

Cynicism was the most radical philosophical school in ancient Greece. It prized individualism and flaunted authority. By attacking social conventions, Cynics strove for self-sufficiency. It is said that when Diogenes, a well-known Cynic, met Alexander the Great and Alexander asked if there was anything he might do for him, Diogenes asked only that the great conqueror would get out of his light.

Cynicism is unbrokenness considerably ripened. Cynicism is a way of controlling one's anger—a toughness of spirit that not only seeks to control one's own emotions but more destructively seeks to control others' perceptions and reactions as well. The cynic is often the "Yes, but . . ." kind of person. They are not downright antagonistic; they simply try to blunt the edge of everyone else around them—everyone but those they can control.

Many of us have been around "Yes, but" people before. They are the ones who add the negatives to a conversation. They often cannot simply affirm another; they affirm with a hefty dose of argumentation thrown in. They feel compelled to bring up opposing points of view. The cynic is a competitor, always trying to level the playing field so that no one else gets an advantage over him—a curmudgeon who seeks to poke holes in others' arguments, seeks to retard the pace of an enterprise through well-timed pessimism, seeks to find faults in others in order to stay ahead of the pack. A cynical attitude is almost the exact opposite of spiritual brokenness.

He seeks to cover another person's weakness.

I recall being told years ago of the ministry of an emerging leader. This particular leader was gaining a great deal of popularity. He was soon to become a great shaker and mover. When I listened to him I detected, quite honestly, areas of pride—and even a dash of arrogance. Rather than responding with a smug, self-satisfied air of superiority, or responding competitively by secretly rejoicing in his character flaws (which would result not only in his own undoing but in one less voice in competition with mine), I, by the grace of God, immediately went into a strong season of prayer. I prayed earnestly for the Lord to be gracious to him and expand his ministry and reveal those things in his life that would become handicaps to him later on. It has been a joy over the last several years to see his ministry emerge and to see some of those very character issues ironed out by God's grace.

The broken person so wants God's reputation to be untarnished that he uses the knowledge of another's weakness as an opportunity to intercede.

He is willing to work for another person's credit.

This test of character strikes deep at our sense of justice. A couple of years ago our two older kids, Cameron and Kelsey, went on a "penny drive." As part of their Sunday school initiative, they canvassed the neighborhoods around our house, gathering pennies for missionaries. Kelsey, our middle child, hit pay dirt in one of the first homes she visited.

She rang the doorbell, explained why she was there, then promptly was given a huge wine jug full of pennies!

Was she ever excited about going to Sunday school the following Sunday! Being close to the same age, Cameron and Kelsey were in the same Sunday school class. Sunday came, and as we pulled into the church parking lot, Kelsey announced that she had to go into the main service for a while and asked her older brother, Cameron, to take the wine jug full of pennies to the Sunday school teacher on her behalf. She said she would follow shortly.

Well, Cameron had just a small bag of pennies. Compared to his sister's stash, his few coins looked pretty paltry. When he walked in with the jug full of pennies, the teacher and all the rest of the kids began to gush over Cameron as if he were the savior of the world. Clearly he was being given credit for a job he had not performed. He was in a quandary, but decided to keep quiet and accept the adulation. When Kelsey got to the Sunday school class and realized that her brother had been given credit for what she had done, she was madder than a hornet! It was so unfair, so unjust! And there was no way she could rectify it, because by the time she got there the class had gone on to other things.

But you can bet that her mother and I got an earful on the drive home. She could not believe that her brother had been so unfair. I knew, though, that God was using that incident to teach Kelsey a valuable lesson—I knew that for what He had planned for her life she was going to need the emotional stamina to be able to work for other people's credit. God was preparing her heart to embrace anonymity with grace.

He is willing to work outside his area of gifting.

For the most part, we are not required to work outside of our aptitudes. Doing that for which we are not gifted can be very frustrating, and generally God will not require that of us. But to keep us from idolizing our gifts or the roles that our gifts create for us, the Lord will ask us at different seasons of our lives to do things that do not come naturally. This not only promotes a greater dependence on Him but keeps us from making our gifts our gods.

He is willing to be second as long as God wants.

The relationship General George Marshall had with Franklin Roosevelt is a testament to the power and influence a second-in-command can have if that position is properly understood and appreciated. Perhaps no other man did more to secure both our victory in World War II as well as the international goodwill we consequently enjoyed than Marshall. He was the architect of the Marshall Plan, which rebuilt Germany in a miraculously short period of time. But his great genius lay in his ability to persuade his commander-in-chief to pursue the most intelligent courses of action.[2]

It is never easy being second. And yet there is as much satisfaction in being second as there is prestige in being first. Though mutual submission in a marriage is the norm, there are times, according to the Scriptures, when the husband must take the lead. Though collegiality can be pursued among a leadership team, there are times when one must take the lead in a given situation. How does the wife feel? How does an associate pastor feel? There is a powerful truth to be understood here. Jesus Himself, no less, modeled what playing second was all about. For in their Trinitarian relations, the Son is co-equal with the Father and the Spirit. But in reference to salvation history, Jesus walked on this earth completely subordinate to the Father. And it was He who accomplished redemption!

Fitting Well

At the end of the day, knowing how to fit in a group is one of life's most important lessons. It is not only basic to our personal happiness, but it enhances our inner sense of freedom. For it is in that place of belonging that we know freedom from loneliness, an inner freedom that comes from knowing that we are accepted. And it is being rightly aligned to authority that rewires us from a bristling, self-focused independence that makes it harder for us to fit with others to a winsome graciousness that has learned the joy—and freedom—of being focused on others.

10

A Marriage Rightly Aligned

For two people in a marriage to live together day after day is unquestionably the one miracle the Vatican has overlooked.

Bill Cosby

Treat yourself and talk to a married couple who have been together over forty years and who love to smile at each other. Amazing sight, isn't it—two gray-haired people, delighting in each other more now than when they walked down the aisle? There is something settling in that smile—like it is possible to finish life with unbroken relationships. Like faithfulness is a more enriching aim than success. Like enduring friendship is not a fantasy.

How are such marriages built?

The apostle Paul shows us the way to a marriage that smiles. In his letter to the Ephesians (5:21–33) he sets forth the most thorough instruction about marriage found in the New Testament. And interestingly enough, much of the secret to a happy marriage lies in an understanding of authority.

Back to the Basics

To better understand how authority works within the marital relationship, let's recall some of our basics. First, only God possesses authority. Second, within the Trinity authority is shared, although there are clear roles and boundaries (such as the Father's headship) that each divine Person expresses. Third, the intent of authority is the creation and nurturing of life; thus, authority is the shared experience of creating and maintaining life. Fourth, to be rightly aligned to authority is to know the privileges and boundaries of each role, just as each person in the Trinity is faithful to His place: the headship of the Father, the word of the Son, the execution of the Spirit.

Based on these guiding principles, I would propose that what we have in Ephesians 5:21–33 is an "authority equation" made up of two people, equal in value, yet who each have a different contribution to that equation. If each understands that difference, peace and harmony should be cultivated more easily. In defining these different contributions, Paul takes his cue from a comparison he draws between Christ and His Bride, the Church. As Jesus and the Church each have specific covenantal roles and responsibilities, so also do the husband and wife.

Many have commented that Paul's discussion of the marital relationship really begins in verse 21: "Submit to one another." There is some truth to this, although here Paul is not speaking of marriage, per se, but of Christian relationships as a whole. Still, it could be argued that the principles of godly relationships certainly should undergird the marriage relationship; so I think the view that verses 22–33 find a foundation in verse 21 is sound. Based on verse 21, therefore, we can say that the husband and the wife share authority in some way.

Mutual submission, however, does not quite nail the subtlety of the marriage dynamic. That is why Paul goes on to specify the differences in the way the husband and wife carry their roles: The husband, Paul says, is the "head"—but this is not the same thing as saying he has full authority over his wife. The wife, Paul says, is to "submit"—but this does not mean unquestioning obedience on her part.

In better understanding these roles, we may be able to see how authority is shared within the marriage relationship: that the husband does not so much hold authority *over* his wife but rather *with* his wife. One might object to this line of thought because it would seem to suggest, overlaying this application on the analogy of Christ and His Church, that the Church's obedience to Christ is a sort of "negotiated cooperation"—as if Christ had to seek the Church's permission or obtain her agreement before giving any commands. But that is not what is meant by "shared authority." There is *one head* of the Church, and that is Christ Jesus. Likewise, there is *one head* in the marital bond, and that is the husband. Paul underscores this in 1 Corinthians 11:3. But if authority is about authoring life *together*, then in both

131

relationships the "head" and the "submitted" contribute to that process.

Perhaps we have looked at these roles—the head and the submitted—through eyes conditioned by past assumptions about authority. Remember the distinction we made in an earlier chapter between "headship" and "authority"? Well, this becomes especially helpful in defining marital roles. There is a leader and a follower in any authority equation. Both have a certain role to fulfill in that equation. In setting these roles in cement, however, we may miss an important relational principle that, if not discerned, can lead to relationships in which we are either controlling or being controlled.

Again, authority is about creating and sustaining life, and both the husband and the wife have a part to play, but in different ways. If the husband is the "head," then we could say that the wife—as the Church is to Christ—is the "responder." Both have an authority. Just as Christ loves and gives Himself up for the Church and invests authority in her, so the husband expresses his headship to his wife by giving himself up for her and giving her authority.

So how can we better understand these roles, what kind of authority does each carry and what are the limits and boundaries to each role?

The Husband's Headship

What does it mean to be the "head"? Again, let's recall ground already covered. First, it means going first—being willing to take the initiative, to take the risks and go out in front.

Second, the head "saves." According to Paul, the husband is the head of the wife. So to "save" her, as the "head," means that he is committed to creating a climate in which the wife is able to rise to her potential. Again, this is what Jesus has done for us. A husband's "headship" does not mean that the wife does not take the lead at times. The acts of "leading" and "following" are not fixed. But the husband's headship does mean that he stewards their teamwork as a couple and ensures that they achieve their aims in the most mutually satisfying way.

Third, the head serves by loving, and loves by dying. According to the Jesus model in Ephesians 5, the head serves through acts of love—sacrificing himself for the sake of the submitted. That is headship. Jesus serves the Church by loving, and loved by dying. Love is an action. The love of Jesus is an act of self-sacrifice. As "head" of the Body, Jesus goes first. As the Scriptures say, "We love Him because He *first* loved us" (1 John 4:19, NKJV, emphasis added). Our response of submission is based on His act of love. So we could say that the *act* precedes the *attitude*. Sometimes we as husbands become impatient with our wives, expecting them to submit just because we are the husbands. But if we expect an *attitude* of submission from our wives (which we will examine when we consider the wife's role), then we need to walk in the *actions* of love.

Like Jesus, a husband exercises headship by serving his wife through laying down his life. How?

- By not demanding compliance, but rather persuading through patient discussion.
- By choosing her over his career if the two become incompatible.

- By focusing on how he can make her feel secure in his love.
- By laying down hobbies and recreation that consistently distract him from spending quality time with her.
- By allowing her opportunity to vent frustration, and suppressing the need to rebut her.

Of course, these are but a few expressions of self-sacrifice. *But these hurt*, you say. Well, yes, death usually does!

The Wife's Submission

Because a husband is the "head" in the marriage relationship does not automatically mean that he possesses the whole picture of authority. "Authority" is the outcome of two parties understanding their contribution. So what about the other role, the "submitted"? First, I would suggest that "submission" is fundamentally an attitude, not an act. Second, it is specifically an attitude of *honoring*, of expressing respect. The Church is submitted to the headship of Christ; we express that submission by honoring Christ, out of which an obedience flows from a trust in His headship—trust, because we know He sacrificed Himself for us. We can obey Him without question because He has perfectly loved us.

But husbands and wives are imperfect people. So we may need to pause here and not stretch the analogy too far.

Headship serves; submissiveness honors. Which comes first? Headship always comes first. That is why it is the head! So serving must precede honoring. As husbands, we cannot expect to be respected by our wives on the one hand if we are not serving in a self-sacrificial way on the other. The way the head and the submitted express their authority is by serving and honoring, respectively: The head *serves*, the submitted *honors*. And to the degree that the head builds trust through his actions of self-sacrificial love, to that degree the wife's heart will be drawn to honor him.

One mistake that I think husbands make is thinking that submission is the act of obedience. No, submission is an *attitude* of honoring. It does not require blind obedience. In fact, when a wife has an honest sense that her husband is making a wrong decision, she is obligated to contribute to the authority equation by coming to him in a respectful manner and pointing that out. A wife can be honest about her disagreements while still being submissive.

When we speak of a wife "obeying" her husband, it should be understood in the context of Jesus and His Church. Jesus does not stand aloof from us, demanding obedience. He has given us His Spirit, who counsels us, comforts us, works in us "to will and to act according to his good purpose" (Philippians 2:13). In other words, Jesus nurtures our obedience. In the same way, a husband should seek to counsel, comfort and help his wife come to a place where they can mutually agree, or at least trust his leadership enough to yield to that leadership when it becomes necessary.

It might seem that we are "strain[ing] out a gnat" (see Matthew 23:24) in being so specific. But sometimes problems emerge in marriages precisely because we have not always defined expectations clearly. For example, a husband might assume that submission is an act and expect his wife to submit to him in everything (see Ephesians 5:24), treating any disagreements from her as insubordination. This can result in the wife feeling like the proverbial "doormat."

On the other hand, the wife may also see submission as an act and feel that she has no voice in the relationship—that she just has to "submit" to her husband's wishes. This may lead her to surmise that she is in a controlling relationship, causing her unnecessary anger. This may further cause her actually to *dishonor* her husband by resisting what she feels is control, thus responding to him—especially at points of disagreement—in a disrespectful manner. Because submission is an attitude, not an act, she should actually find herself free to disagree—but in an honoring way.

Though it is true that the husband's self-sacrifice should engender the wife's submission, it is also true that the wife should have a submissive attitude toward her husband because of the role of her husband's headship, not because he "sacrificed" sufficiently. Peter's encouragement that the wife's submissiveness could perhaps win an unsaved husband (see 1 Peter 3:1–2) makes sense only if we understand that the wife's call to submit to her husband is a call to honor the *role of the husband*, whether or not he is fulfilling his responsibilities.

By better defining our terms we can come to some important conclusions. In this case, simply by seeing submission more as an attitude than an act, we can conclude that:

- The husband does not have authority over his wife— they both have authority within the marriage relationship appropriate to their roles.
- The husband is the "head." But headship is not about how to wield power; it is about taking the lead in creating an environment in which they, as a couple, can experience satisfying teamwork.

- The husband should not expect blind obedience—but he can expect to be honored as the head.
- The wife has a right to expect her husband to exercise his headship by sacrificing his life—his wants and preferences—for her sake. But she should also realize that she is to respond to his role as head with a submissive attitude.

Let's look at the wife's role more closely. In verse 24, the wife is instructed to submit to her husband in everything. Now some wives might object, "Well, that leaves little room for disagreement; it sounds to me like we're back to the old 'doormat' arrangement." This is where we need to come back and remember that submission is not so much an act but an attitude. To be submissive in everything, even when registering disagreements, is to show respect for the husband by expressing those disagreements in an honoring rather than combative way.

For example, if a wife becomes alarmed at a direction the husband is taking—say, investing their retirement income in a risky venture (which should not be the case anyway, for if the husband were loving his wife well he would have included her in the decision in the first place)—then she shares her disagreement in a respectful way. "I do appreciate your looking after our finances, and all the research you've done, but I'm uneasy with this particular investment. Can you explain it better to me? Maybe there's something I'm not seeing." If after discussing the issue the wife is still uneasy, she might say, "You know I respect you, but this is a huge amount of money and I really feel we need to get outside financial advice from an investment counselor."

If the husband still does not listen, then the wife should weigh the consequences: Will yielding to her husband primarily affect only her? Or might there be consequences that would affect others, like the children? This is an important distinction to make. If it is only her preferences that are at stake, she needs to ask another question: Does her husband routinely ignore her advice? If so, he is not functioning in "headship," meaning that he lays down his life by taking his wife's judgments seriously. Most likely that pattern signals that it is time for outside counsel. However, if he does usually listen to his wife, but in this particular situation is determined to go ahead, then the wife should consider yielding on this point. That is the "honoring" position, which is to give his headship the benefit of the doubt. Yet if his decision could directly affect others and he refuses to listen to her, then she should seek counsel from someone in spiritual authority, such as their pastor.

Two Needs

The two primary roles in the authority equation—the head and the submitted—correspond to primordial needs in both the man and the woman. The nesting instinct of the woman creates within her a deep bent toward *security*. The hunter instinct in the man causes him to define himself by his achievements, which makes him highly purpose driven. Thus, we could say that the deep bent in the man is *destiny*. Because the man is ultimately focused on destiny, *respect* is his most felt need. Because the woman is focused on security, her most felt need is *love*.

That is why Paul encourages the husband to love and the wife to submit, or honor. The wife, through submitting, not only feeds his need for respect, which should inspire hope for his destiny—she is creating a reservoir of love that she will receive in return, which should deepen her sense of security. Likewise, the husband taking the lead and loving first—even before he feels honored—creates this same dynamic in reverse. By loving his wife he fosters a climate in which he should increasingly be respected. As Paul says, "He who loves his wife loves himself" (Ephesians 5:28). Each one's response feeds the other's needs.

In the husband's little dividend—that by loving his wife he loves himself—is a sweet paradox often missed. A wife yielding to her husband is actually returning to his side, fulfilling the ancient mystery of her origins. God could have created the woman out of dust like He did the man. But God took her from Adam. Man's bent toward work speaks to his origins, the earth. A woman's bent toward a man reflects her origins, the man's rib cage. The woman the man chooses to marry becomes more than a "helpmeet," or partner. She becomes the missing part of him. As a husband, think of what fulfills you the most: A hobby, such as golf? Receiving accolades at work? Seeing your kids follow in your footsteps? *The number one investment a husband makes in his personal fulfillment is caring for his wife.* Like no other activity you could do, tending your bride is the primary way God has designed for you to feel good about yourself. Thus, a husband who cares for and tends to his wife lives in the greatest possible fulfillment.

Because the woman is in the "responder" position, her felt need for security is going to create a further need for *communication.* And one of the ways the husband shows love toward his wife is in making communication with her one of his highest priorities. Christ's sacrificial love is evidenced by the fact that, in that sacrifice, he fully communicated Himself. If the husband is truly to love his wife as Christ loves the Church, it means that he will spend as much time in developing a good environment of communication within his marriage as he does in, say, his job or with his buddies.

Sometimes a husband can tend to see his wife's need for communication as getting in the way of his ability to accomplish his goals, whether in career promotion or golfing with the boys. His impatience is often expressed with "I don't have the time; I'm too busy making an income. Surely she sees that as a sign of my love for her."

What the husband often fails to recognize is that her need for communication goes beyond just a need; *it goes to the essence of the man's part in the authority equation.* As head, he serves by sacrificing himself. Communication may not come easy, but it is not about easy—it is about sacrifice. Self-sacrifice is never easy! But self-sacrifice is the key to the effective exercise of his headship. If he does not exercise his headship properly, in the spirit of self-sacrifice, he forfeits his place of authority.

There is an intriguing subtext to Paul's observation that a man, by loving his wife, loves his own self. The very things that many husbands fear—vulnerability and communication—are the very things that actually authenticate their manhood, their selfhood. The correct exercise of their headship produces a sense of masculine self-respect. In fact, exercising proper headship should cause the fitting response in the wife—respect. And that is the very thing he needs!

Coping Mechanisms

Not only do the "head" and the "responder" each have a unique part in the authority equation, each also has a primary coping mechanism to which they will resort in an effort to protect themselves. If they feel that their concerns are being ignored, or that they are losing leverage in the relationship, they will respond in ways that reflect their particular roles.

For example, the wife as responder is called to express an attitude of submissiveness to her husband. But the "submitter" in the authority equation will often feel less powerful; and to the degree that she feels powerless she risks slipping into the most detrimental coping mechanism the less powerful have: *the attempt to control*, often through manipulation. The old saying, "If Mamma ain't happy, ain't nobody happy!" reveals where the seat of power is in some marriages. A wife who does not understand the wisdom—and the freedom—of submission will tend to exhibit controlling behaviors like manipulation.

By contrast, the husband, remember, is called to love his wife as Christ loved the Church. Love, as we have said, is an action—so what the husband has to avoid when he feels threatened is to stop acting in a loving manner, which is *withdrawal*.

The one who is the head is the one called to serve, and the ungodly response of the server is withdrawing. The one who is submitting is called to honor, yet out of her sense of powerlessness she can tend to control. The great fear of the head is rejection; the great fear of the one submitting is being controlled. So often the head deals with his rejection by rejecting; the submitter deals with her fear of being controlled by controlling.

There is an added encouragement for the submitted. In Ephesians 5:22, wives are encouraged to cultivate an attitude of respect and honor toward their husband *as to the Lord.* This should be a great comfort. It is a part of the justice of God that those called to submit are given the opportunity of a greater sensitivity to "divine revelation" if they but receive it and walk in it. What Paul is saying is that as tough as submissiveness may be at times, wives are given a chance to have an inner revelation of their act of submissiveness as that being directed toward the Lord. In other words, Christ is extending to the wife the power to see her submissiveness as a love response to Jesus—and seeing her submission in these terms can actually keep her from feeling controlled.

So let's summarize what we have discovered thus far. The wife is

- called to walk in an attitude of submissiveness;
- which is expressed in respecting and honoring her husband;
- which *can* mean that she is the less powerful one in the authority equation;
- and which further means that she has to avoid becoming controlling;
- but which also means that she can know a keener sense of God's presence.

The husband is

- called to take the leadership through acts of love;
- which creates a climate in which the wife can *safely* submit;

- which releases the wife to express an attitude of honor toward him;
- but which also means that if he feels disrespected, he cannot use his power to withdraw;
- which further means that although his is the more powerful role in the authority equation, God's justice ensures that he will come under stricter judgment;
- and because of his greater power, he risks having less sensitivity to the Lord's presence if he does not love his wife as Christ loves the Church.

The authority of each marriage partner begins to wane to the degree that the wife controls and the husband withdraws. If both partners are polarizing, remember: *The head always has to go first.* If the wife exhibits controlling behaviors, it is because there is a deep sense of insecurity. The husband should not read this as a wife trying to control him. Rather, he should read this that his wife is feeling insecure. That is why the head needs to act with love even in the face of potential rejection. That is the way Christ loved the Church. It is not a conditional love; it is unconditional. But if the husband withdraws and does not act in love in order to cultivate his wife's response of submissiveness in return, then he needs to own the lion's share of the consequences of the relationship breakdown.

A Lack of Grace

A controlling response from a wife shows that she lacks a fundamental understanding of grace. A withdrawal response on the part of a husband shows an equal lack of understanding. But they lack understandings of grace in different ways. By controlling, the wife is saying that she does not trust the power of God extended to us by His grace to intervene in a situation. The husband who withdraws shows a fundamental lack of understanding of grace in that he has not grasped unconditional acceptance.

As the French writer André Maurois once observed, "A happy marriage is a long conversation which always seems too short." The long conversation is nurtured by two people who have become two friends, free to be friends because they know how they fit together. And they know how to fit together because they have long since valued the boundaries that are set in place through a good grasp of authority.

A person who has never fully seen himself physically cannot fully appreciate who he is. He needs a mirror. The first time he sees himself in a mirror, he finds a new freedom that comes from greater self-awareness. Freedom is not having it our own way in a marriage. Freedom is the discovery of our own selves that cannot be had unless we have the "mirror" of another.

11

The Five Basics of Authority

> Authority without wisdom is like a heavy ax without an edge, fitter to bruise than polish.
>
> Anne Bradstreet (seventeenth-century poet)

Not long ago I took a walk in a nearby park. Enjoying the warm spring day, I decided to catch a breather on a bench and people-watch for a while. Soon I noticed a family strolling down the path, young parents with kids ranging from a little one in a stroller to two boys probably around ages three and five. The two boys were bringing up the rear, the five-year-old leading his younger brother along. All at once the younger boy bolted out in front. This peeved the older brother, and he yelled, "No, *I'm* the leader!" then ran in front to retake his position of leadership. Well, the three-year-old was not about to stay in tow for long, so he raced ahead again—to which the older one responded with greater agitation, "*I'm* the leader!" Clearly the five-year-old was not about to let this upstart upstage him. But the three-year-old could not have cared less about his brother's insecurity. He continued to challenge the elder's "leadership" until Dad finally had to step in and settle the issue.

The question of "Who's the leader?" is as central to understanding how authority frees me as are questions of my own attitudes and fears. If figuring out the "leadership arrangement" was critical to these boys' happiness, then it must be pretty central to ours.

Up to this point we have been talking about authority, boundaries and submission in fairly personal terms: how we as believers walk in personal authority, how we handle boundaries, how understanding authority impacts our relationships. And our main point throughout has been that *understanding authority brings us into personal freedom.*

But now we need to segue to a sphere beyond ourselves—for, as believers, we are part of the Church, members of Christ's Body. Here the authority issue revolves around not just my freedom but the freedom of those to whom I am committed. We are moving from a focus on the individual to a focus on the group, in this case the Church. And wherever groups function, the dynamics of *authority* cannot help but drift into issues of *leadership.* Understanding the concept of leadership and how leaders are supposed to handle authority, what to do if they are not handling it well, how we respond to leaders in a biblically submissive manner—these questions about authority are as vital to our personal freedom as are the personal boundaries we have discussed earlier.

Watching these two young lads dicker over position reminded me that most people view authority in terms of position and power. But is this God's view of authority? And again, what does God's nature tell us about authority?

We need to do some more theology, so hang in there. For by seeing "authority" through the lens of God's model we will be able to glean principles that may reshape our thinking about leadership, as well as mute a good deal of the fear some may have of those in positions of authority. Here we will look at five of these principles.

Principle #1: Only God has authority.

There is an assumption that we need to identify in regard to authority if we are to understand it rightly: *Only God ultimately possesses authority.* All other authority is delegated. We cannot say in an absolute sense that a given person has authority in a particular structure, or that the government has a certain authority over us, or even that in a democracy authority is vested in the people. For in reality any constructs of human systems or organizations are merely channels of God's authority. No one really "has" authority, in the sense of owning it.

The reason why only God possesses authority is because He is the only one who knows everything. To possess absolute authority, one has to possess total knowledge. God, of course, knows the end from the beginning, and that is why only He can truly "have" authority. And because He knows the end from the beginning, there is nothing that can threaten His authority. Because God can never be threatened, He does not have to coerce through threats or cajole through bribes. He is free to influence by love.

In my book *I Am: The Unveiling of God*, I use the Garden of Eden story to describe how—given the fact that we *do not* possess absolute knowledge—the illegitimate grasping of authority plays out in the unraveling of our lives. I show how Adam and Eve usurped an authority they could not handle and were thus forced to assume responsibilities for which they were not designed. The problem was that since they did not know the end from the beginning, they had to protect themselves from what they did not know. To protect themselves, they developed devices of self-preservation that have come to be known as rights—mandatory mechanisms of defense in a selfish world. Over time these defenses become the rights by which we attempt to guarantee our satisfaction: the right to privacy, the right to happiness, the right to be understood, the right to succeed, the right to be vindicated when we are the victims of injustice. And ever since the Garden, people have asserted their rights in a grim tug-of-war of selfishness that constantly rips at the fabric of the relationships for which we yearn.[1]

So we see, in the final analysis, that only God truly "possesses" authority. Any authority that we exercise is merely delegated by Him.

Principle #2: Leadership is not "earned" through servanthood; leadership *is* servanthood.

Much of what shapes our leadership styles is borrowed from secular models—models that often stress the achievement of goals, the increase of productivity and a view of people as resources to be directed toward the accomplishment of desired ends. But think for a moment of eternity past when nothing yet had been created: no angels, no planets, nothing. When there was no one but God—Father, Son and Holy Spirit—who was the leader? To conceive of the Godhead as some kind of hierarchy would be inappropriate! To imagine the Father as the Chairman of the Board, the Son as the Chief Executive Officer and the Holy Spirit as the Chief Operating Officer is to misperceive greatly the nature of the Godhead. Again, the Three are co-equal, co-eternal and co-essential.

What might this tell us about leadership? It shows that in eternity past—when there was no one else but God—there was no leadership function, as we understand it, in the Godhead. But in their love for one another, the Father always *served* the Son and the Spirit, the Son always *served* the Father and the Spirit, and the Spirit always *served* the Father and the Son. In other words, *servanthood has always existed.* The function of leadership was not necessary until Creation.

This should radically adjust our value system in regard to how we view leadership. *Leadership is merely a created function, whereas servanthood is an eternal reality!* Our culture tends to place a premium on leadership; God seems to place the accent on servanthood. Even with all our efforts at cultivating humility, we still tend to dichotomize this servanthood/leadership issue in such a way that servanthood is perceived as merely the necessary requisite for leadership. "If I prove myself to be a good servant, then I'll get to be a leader." We tend to see leadership as the graduation from servanthood—servanthood as a compulsory discipline, leadership as a treasured privilege.

Trying to cultivate an appetite for servanthood through the exercise of humility may not go far enough. We must undergo a more thorough change in our assumptions about God and how He works, which in turn will inform and radically alter our value system. I recall reading, a few years ago, a bestselling book on leadership and management that made quite a case for the servant-leader model. But the author's slant revealed his bias, for his call to model servanthood was based on a need to earn the right to lead—which seems pretty noble, after all, until such an assumption is scrutinized more closely. For this author, as for most of us, servanthood was a *means* to something. We may sincerely don the cloak of servanthood, but all too often we do so as a means of earning trust, as a persona we employ to garner followings rather than as a conviction that permanently shapes our lifestyles, as a way of exercising effective leadership rather than the definition of leadership itself.

In buying into the distorted idea of "serving in order to earn the right to lead" we are subconsciously using the veneer of servanthood to gain a place for ourselves. With this attitude our appetite for servanthood most certainly will wane over time, leaving us vulnerable to the temptations of being manipulative, driven, suspicious and resentful when people do not fulfill our expectations.

The idea of "leading after serving" does not go far enough. We must undergo a thorough change in our value system by seeing this issue through the lens of God's nature. We may have the desire to reflect Christ by being godly servants, but unless our values have been transformed we will not have the power to walk as servants! Seen against the backdrop of His nature, it is not a matter of leading *after* serving—because leading *is* serving.

Principle #3: Authority is more about tending relationships than holding positions.

Divine authority flows from who God is. And God is a communion of three Persons who have perfectly and eternally loved each other. If it is prudent to be cautious about viewing the Trinity as a permanent hierarchy, then authority—as the Trinity expresses it—should be defined initially by the mutuality and relationship that the Three enjoy.

This highlights a foundational truth: *Authority, as it is modeled for us in the Trinity, is first a relational concept.* This is not to say that authority cannot be positional, but that reality is secondary. And because God's authority is first relational, and meant to express the permanence of love, we can conclude that the exercise of all authority is meant to be understood as the means of preserving that love.

If we rightly understand this, then submission to God's delegated authorities and the yielding of our lives to biblical boundaries should never feel threatening to us. For in the final analysis, submission to authority moves us toward love; rebellion against authority separates us from love.

In a previous chapter we talked about the idea of the "monarchy of the Father." While this view is supported by the biblical story, overemphasis may also lead to church structures that are too authoritarian. If the Godhead is understood primarily as the One (Father) as source of the other

Two (Son and Spirit), this *may* lead to justifying the idea of one leader exercising unilateral authority over the many.

On the other hand, if, in a desire to promote more democratic systems, we "flatten" an understanding of the Trinity in which the co-equality is overly stressed, this may lead to structures in which there is no identifiable leader. This can lead, then, to power struggles in which people constantly jockey for position.

So how do we muddle through this theological maze and come to some understanding—imperfect as it may be—of the Godhead?

Theologians make a distinction between how the three Persons function in their relations with each other within the Godhead ("intra-Trinitarian relations") and how they "team together," as it were, in their missions ("inter-Trinitarian relations"). As we saw earlier, Scripture records that the Godhead has been active in two primary missions: creation and redemption. When it comes to their *missions*, the Three have different functions and can be seen as operating in a sort of chain of command. Hence we see, for example, the Son expressing obedience to the Father. But when it comes to their *relationship*, the Three are equal.

It is here that we make a fundamental mistake in regard to church systems and structures: We confuse "relationship" and "mission." We will touch on this in a later chapter, but let's draw an implication from this now. When it comes to a task—say, your church puts on a children's musical—there should be a leader for that task. Those who want to be involved will need to be willing to lock into a certain chain of command so that boundaries, roles and expectations can be clearly defined and the task accomplished well. The leader will naturally relate to that team in a directive way. The subordinates will need to yield to this "authority structure" with grace in order to get the job done.

The challenge is how this team relates to each other when not on task, or when the task is done. Here it is all too easy for leaders—especially if they have more permanent, executive-type roles—to continue to relate to those people as if they were in a chain of command, with the expectations of compliance that come with that. When this happens, people can feel less valued, even demeaned, because they feel that their value as people is only as important as the functions they carry out. This is what I mean when I say that leaders can, quite innocently, confuse relationship with mission.

God is eternal relationship. And genuine authority flows from the commitment to tend our relationships well. Because of this, we can look at each other differently and value each other equally, though we *do* have different functions.

Principle #4: Authority is based in integrity and humility.

The authority that God exercises is based in the fact that not only do the Father, Son and Spirit eternally love each other, but they will be eternally true to that nature of mutual love. In other words, *God's authority is based in the fact that He manifests integrity*. God is not only perfect love, but He is unchanging; He is genuine. That God is faithful to who He is brings us to another proposition about authority: *Authority flows from personal integrity.* Being honest to oneself. No masks, no pretenses. *Character.*

Authority, therefore, is not just a relational concept but a moral one as well, in that it is a matter of integrity to be faithful to His nature of unselfish love. God's authority is evident from the fact that He is faithful to who He is.

If "authority" at its essence is both a moral and relational—not positional—concept, then the manner in which authority is expressed and exercised in and through any institution—be it family, church, government or business—must follow suit. The implications that ensue from these propositions as to how authority is defined and exercised are critical, and we will consider a couple of them.

First, to be a person of authority is to be a person of integrity. For instance, to have integrity is to be, among other things, faithful to who we are in the sense of the way God designed us. To be thus is both to be freed from the crowding of others' expectations as well as to affirm the dignity of every person. In this sense, authority is not the prerogative of leadership but the moral quality of faithfulness in which *all*—regardless of the size or breadth of one's influence or function—can excel and sense equal value from the Lord.

Second, to have integrity—following God's example—is to have integrity in our relationships. This does not just mean treating the other guy right. It is much deeper than that. It is being healthily interdependent. We see in the Trinity an ease with which the Three move in concert with each other. There is no striving among them, but rather a perfect synchronization of roles. And in this way the Godhead models humility. As we have already seen, humility is foundational to authority. A team that is willing to be interdependent is a team that shows that they have a good grasp of humility.

A key to developing interdependence is the truth that there is an "authority" in every function. Theologians discuss a concept that may at first sound esoteric. They talk about the truth that God the Father *is* God the Father *because* there is God the Son. In other words, the members of the Godhead need each other, in a way, because it is as they interact together that each Person's unique place within the Trinity is defined. The Son cannot be the Son without the Father.

In contemporary treatments of leadership and management, consultants speak of an authority of the leader and an authority of the follower. Instead of seeing that authority is about humility, character and rightly relating to others, we are used to thinking of authority as a positional concept: People "have" authority over others. This kind of thinking exposes a worldly understanding of authority. Yet if we in the Body of Christ understand authority in relational terms, *every person* has authority.

This has profound consequence and underscores how much we need each other. The leader obviously has a more direct kind of authority. But the follower has a unique authority as well: the authority of influence. For there is no leader without a follower. It is, in a sense, the follower that constitutes the leader. The leader carries an authority that calls people to function together well—it is a *functional* authority. But the follower has an authority by virtue of his or her willingness to follow, which actually enforces the truth that everyone is of equal value. If a leader ceases to be a leader who walks in humility and tends relationships well, he no longer commands genuine authority. He may hold power, but he does not carry authority.

The bottom-line understanding that *everyone* is of *equal* value becomes the dominant way in which we think of authority. And the wise leader will not confuse his function as a leader to coordinate the functions of his followers with his call to ensure that all under his care will feel equally respected.

Principle #5: Authority is measured by faithfulness.

As we have seen, authority is based in integrity, and a large part of being a person of integrity is being *faithful* to what we have been given, stewarding well what we already have. Jesus taught that if we are faithful in little we will be given grace to be faithful in much. Because the world's system frames authority in terms of position and power, we often think that to have more authority means gaining a more powerful position. Jesus turns that whole mindset on its head in the Parable of the Talents (see Matthew 25:14–30), which gives us an understanding of how God views authority.

In the story, Jesus tells of a master who gave three of his servants money to invest: to one five talents, to another two talents, to another one talent. He then left for a long journey. Upon his return, he summoned his servants to give an account of what they had done with the talents given them. We recall, of course, that the servant to whom the one talent was given did nothing with that talent and consequently incurred the wrath of the master. But the other two doubled their master's investment, and in this we see a very important truth about authority.

Though one servant was given five talents and the other two, this is not the same as saying that the one with more talents had more authority. The fact is that both servants doubled their master's income. They both exhibited the same authority to achieve capital gains, though they managed different amounts. For example, let's say I had one hundred dollars and put fifty dollars in a mutual fund company with one million dollars in assets and the other fifty dollars in a mutual fund with one billion dollars in assets. And let's assume that at the end of five years they both had doubled my investment. Does it matter to me whether one mutual fund company was bigger than the other? No, the "authority" of each company to handle my investments well was equal, measured by the fact that they both returned 100 percent on my principal.

This is the way God looks at authority! Authority is not about breadth of scope, significance of position or size of influence; it is about being faithful with what God has given us. We may look at a leader like Billy Graham, see the vast reach of his ministry and conclude that when we all get to heaven he is going to have much more authority than the rest of us. But that is not the way God views authority. If you are a second-grade teacher and you are faithful to the "field" or "measure" you have been given, you will have just as much authority when you get to heaven as the person who has been president of a denomination.

If we see authority from God's point of view, we will be less likely to be envious of another person's "measure" and more motivated to maximize what *we* have been given, knowing that authority is released proportionate to faithfulness. And if we have understood this, we will not be apt to grasp for leadership positions.

Conclusion

Where genuine authority is being expressed within a team of leaders, or any group of believers for that matter, you will see an environment (1) in which each is excelling in his or her gifts as the consequence of the belief that the true essence of authority is integrity and (2) that engenders a sense of mutual respect. If we all walk within our "divine design," we will be equal in authority. In fact, one of the signs that a ministry is manifesting biblical authority is the culture of mutual respect evident in that ministry. Misunderstanding here breeds an environment in which people are easily hurt. When concepts and uses of authority demean others, or make others feel inferior, they run counter to the very essence of authority as expressed in the Godhead.

Perhaps our struggles with authority could be eased if we saw that authority and respect were symbiotic. A community of believers who feel deep mutual respect, though their individual roles may be vastly different, reveals the presence of leaders who have truly understood the dynamics of authority. Success and productivity do not adequately assess true spiritual authority. Honor and respect that arise from acknowledging the integrity of others as they walk true to their design—*that's the measure of authority.*

12

The "S" Word

My defenses were so great. The cocky rock and roll hero who knows all the answers was actually a terrified guy who didn't know how to cry.

John Lennon

A veteran missionary who had served in China for part of her career once told me this story. As she was strolling through her village, she saw a man in a small shanty on the side of the road beating something. As she drew closer she saw that he was pounding on a piece of cold sheet metal. He was obviously trying to shape it into something, but was using no fire or any other source of heat to make the metal malleable. Using a rather large mallet, he just kept pounding and pounding.

This went on for quite a long time, until the metal began to bend and bow a bit. When it did, he began to take smaller mallets of various sizes and hammered more gently. As it began to take shape, he began tapping the piece with the smallest mallets, smoothing the sides as he did. Soon a sturdy wok sat on the craftsman's block, its sides smooth and shiny, with barely a trace of the hammer's incessant pounding.

The missionary was amazed that all this shaping was produced without a fire or a furnace—just the pounding and tapping of various hammers. She recounted that as she mused on this scene the Lord began to speak to her and said, *The quicker you yield to Me, girl, the easier the hammering.* She knew what God was trying to say through this living parable. First, by yielding to the Master's hand, she would avoid the unnecessary fires of testing. Second, by submitting to His Lordship wholeheartedly, the quicker she "bent and bowed" to the Master's will, the less "pounding" she would incur and the quicker the Master could "tap" her into Christlikeness.

We often think the Lord has to put us in the "furnace of affliction" to test us. I suggest that we do not always need the furnace of affliction—we just need to submit to the hammering quickly so that we can bend in the Master's hand.

Of course most of us would say that we have no problem submitting to God's authority; it's people's authority we struggle with—especially if we are under it! But remember, authority is the "right to author," and God has exclusive rights to write the script for anyone's life. If authority is the right to author, then to be rightly aligned to authority is to recognize God's authorship. Some He equips to lead in certain situations, others to follow. Some may lead in one setting, then follow in another. Those who follow well are often given opportunities of leadership, albeit roles that are equal to their skills.

We may at times struggle with those who are given authority over us, but we need to remember that submission to authority is recognizing that God has authored that authority in a person or a group of persons—and that to submit to that authority is not an act of subservience to a leader but an expression of obedience to the Lord. That is why Paul could encourage those who were slaves to "obey those who are your masters on earth. . . . Do your work heartily, as for the Lord rather than for men" (Colossians 3:22–23, NASB).

Understanding Submission

God often "taps us into Christlikeness" through others, especially those who are in roles of authority over us. The dreaded word *submission* need not strike a chord of fear within us. Rather, to understand submission is to understand both the character adjustments this word calls for as well as the safety it provides. The word *submit* means "to be arranged under another."[1] If we trust the sovereignty of God, then His arrangement is our assignment. To not submit to an authority God has arranged us under is to resist God's assignment.

Peter has some very pertinent things to say about submission to authority in 1 Peter 2:13–3:7. He begins with a stark injunction: "Submit yourselves for the Lord's sake to every human institution, whether to a king as the one in authority, or to governors as sent by him" (NASB). What makes Peter's command so stunning is that he is writing this letter while under the rule of Nero, one of the most profane and sadistic Roman emperors. For Peter to require this of his fellow believers, knowing they were under such a tyrant, says something about the importance Peter placed on this concept of submission to authority.

The key to these opening verses in Peter's discussion of submission is the phrase "for the Lord's sake." When we read this passage it seems that the requirements Peter lays out are just too difficult, if not unfair. But again, to "submit" is to say yes to God's assignment.

Jacob had an assignment that was quite challenging. To be told by your employer (who was also his uncle—a double whammy) that you had to work for him seven years just to marry the girl of your dreams may seem awfully demanding. But when Laban pulls a trick—getting Jacob to marry the girl's sister and then telling him that he has to work another seven years for the right to marry his chosen—this seems to warrant a lawsuit!

But God was in this; it was an *assignment*. And not only was it for the Lord's sake—as it prepared Jacob to be the patriarch God had destined him to be—but it turned out well for Jacob, too. He was able to acquire massive assets while under the protection of his uncle, creating great wealth for himself with very little risk. God's assignment that Jacob endure a long season under an unscrupulous uncle turned out to be one of the most important assignments of his life.

What is done for the Lord's sake turns out to be for our sake, too! As with the word *authority*, by which the Lord wants us to hear "love" and "freedom," so it is with the word *submission*: God wants us to know the importance and value of the words *priority*, *order* and *protection*. If we can catch this and undergo a change in our thinking, we will better understand the benefits of submitting to authority.

To help us shift our mindset about submission, let's look at four insights.

Insight #1

The first is this: *Submission is about yielding to the "order of things."* As we saw earlier, we live with limits. They are all around us. Time is one of the most unyielding limits we experience. It will not rewind for us, nor make up for what we squander of it. Our bodies are another inflexible limit. Try as we might to master multitasking, we just will not be able to do everything at once. And because we cannot do everything at once, we have to *prioritize*. Recognizing our temporal and physical boundaries helps us "order" ourselves and manage our world in the safest, healthiest way. If we violate the natural order of our bodily need for sleep, for instance, our health will break down. By yielding to right order—including the people whom God has placed over us—we will cultivate the wisdom to manage our lives better through establishing right priorities, which in our helter-skelter culture has become a most critical issue.

As an illustration, when a soldier is seriously wounded on the battlefield, the medic has to choose what he treats first. He has to stop the bleeding before tending to the soldier's broken leg. He has to "prioritize." When faced with a situation demanding immediate triage, how does the medic instinctively know what his priorities should be? It goes back to a prior response of submission. The medic's willingness to submit to superiors during training gives him the inner script to respond well automatically to the limits and boundaries the battlefield presents to him. His ability to make critical decisions when it counts comes from having already developed a pattern of submitting to authority. Learning to submit to the authorities God places over us actually equips us to walk in wisdom in everyday life.

Insight #2

But not only does submission to authority prepare the medic to prioritize effectively, it establishes a lifestyle of rightly referencing to authority that ultimately equips the medic to save lives. And this leads us to a second insight: *Submission to authority is meant to create an environment of safety, not control.* By allowing time-tested medical procedures to determine his course of action, the medic is essentially placing himself "under" the authority of that knowledge. On the battlefield, he does not debate the procedures, he does not question them—he immediately places himself under that authority. Now there is room for his personal judgment within the parameters of established medical practice, but he does not decide each time he treats a wounded soldier whether to follow those procedures. And because he has walked well under authority in his training, lives are saved.

You might say, "So he doesn't question medical procedures. But what if medical understanding is wrong at a given time—like the practice of bleeding patients was two hundred years ago?" If there is a consistent pattern of harmful results that stem from a given medical practice, the procedures must be questioned and tested. We should respond similarly to systems of government that are destructive. For example, we should resist and withdraw from totalitarian regimes that violate human rights. But even here we must make a careful distinction between *moral* resistance and *violent* resistance. Jesus turned the money changers' tables upside down as an act of moral outrage, but he refused to allow Peter to wield the sword against the arresting officers in Gethsemane.

We should also make a careful distinction between properly *withdrawing* from illegitimate authority and *overthrowing* that authority. It can be argued that we can discern biblical procedures that allow us to withdraw from authority. For example, we see this in David's situation when he withdrew from Saul. But withdrawing from an authority is not overthrow. This subtle but important distinction in some ways spells the difference between the American and French revolutions. It is an argument that goes well beyond our boundaries here, but, simply put, we could propose that the American Revolution was based in a desire not to overthrow the British monarchy but rather simply to withdraw from it. The French Revolution, on the other hand, was aimed at destroying the monarchy. There is no basis in Scripture whereby we are given permission to overthrow authority.

Insight #3

But question authority we can. And though we will consider the biblical guidelines for this more thoroughly in a later chapter, we can summarize here a third insight about submission: *If we do question authority, we are to do so in an honoring manner.*

Many schoolchildren will remember the story of Louis Pasteur and his bravery in the face of unjust criticism. When attempting to disprove the long-held scientific theory of spontaneous generation, he endured the skepticism of many of his colleagues. But the reaction of the "scientific authorities" did not dissuade Pasteur from finally proving this theory false. And because he rightly questioned—and ultimately debunked—an accepted scientific position, he was able to open the door to a whole new understanding of microbiology, which led to the development of vaccines for many diseases like rabies.

Pasteur questioned, but he did so within the boundaries of humility and deference to his contemporaries. He used the well-established scientific methods of his day to come to new conclusions about the cause of disease. He did not just state his opinions; he proved his theory through accepted scientific processes. In this way he honored his colleagues.

This tells us something about how we question in a submissive manner. If something needs to be changed, we should seek to do so, whenever possible, through legitimate means—through methods that already have been recognized by the people needing the change. When it comes to changing our government, for example, we do so through the ballot box, not the pointed gun. The systems of getting propositions on the ballot and voting for a candidate are the methods that have been recognized by the American people as those to effect change.

Sometimes we find ourselves in conflict with an authority figure. We will devote more time to this in a later chapter. Suffice it to say that rendering honor, which Fawn Parish states is the way we "love well,"[2] is a key to handling such conflicts.

Insight #4

We would do well to remember the fourth insight. Submission, as we have said, is yielding to the right order of things. But we need to acknowledge this: *Our own minds cannot be the final judge of what "order" is.* For example, a teenager cannot be in charge of regulating his sleep regimen. He needs outside counsel. This is true with all of us. Most college kids I know throw sleep to the wind—but eventually that catches up with them. There have to be boundaries.

If each individual determines what is true for himself, basically we create a society like Israel experienced in the time of the judges: "Everyone did what was right in his own eyes" (Judges 21:25, NASB). This can lead only to chaos. My friend Mike Riches, who pastored for many years, makes an astute observation when he says that Judges 21:25 is the background to 1 Samuel 3:1, which says, "The word of the LORD was rare in those days" (NKJV). Because all the people did what was right in their own eyes, they grew dull to the voice of the Lord. Over time, individual autonomy leads to social disharmony—and divine silence.

The Two Sides of Submission

When looking at authority passages in the New Testament, we will often find the truth cutting both ways: a call to submit to legitimate authority and a warning for those wielding authority to handle it humbly. This is the "authority equation" to which I referred earlier. We tend to think of authority in terms of those who have it and those who are under it. But from a biblical standpoint this just is not the case. It is better to see the exercise of authority as the outcome of two dynamics: those called in a situation to create life-giving environments and those called to express honor. We might further simplify this to *serving* and *honoring*.

Those who exercise headship in a given relationship have been given authority, but remember: Authority is the "right to author"—which, again, means it is about creating rather than destroying. One of the main words for "authority" in the Greek of the New Testament is *exousia*. This word lays the stress on building up, not tearing down. Paul puts the emphasis here, as well, in the passage that contains his most ardent defense of his apostleship. Twice in 2 Corinthians 10–13 Paul says that the authority God gave him was for building up, not tearing down (10:8; 13:10).

So in the authority equation the one exercising headship serves by creating an environment for those under his headship that is life giving—a climate of safety and joy, in which they can develop their potential and in which necessary correction need not be feared. The one under the headship of another makes an equally important contribution to the authority equation. He is called to create an environment of honor: knowing how to question directives in a respectful manner, affirming the role the leader is carrying, being pliable in the face of what may appear to be unreasonable demands (see 1 Peter 2:18–20).

Both parties thus create an environment that flows wherever true authority is given place—an environment of order and peace. Authority is a sword that cuts both ways. One side of the blade calls those in authority to account: Are they truly serving those they lead? The other side of the blade calls those under authority to account: Are they honoring those over them in the Lord?

This "sword" is seen in many passages of the New Testament. For example, in 1 Peter 2:21–23 Peter exhorts us to submit as Jesus submitted. He hinges his entire discussion about submission to authority (people to the civil authorities, servants to masters, spouses to each other) upon Christ's example, as if he means to convey to both leader and follower alike that if the Lord we serve walked in humble submission, how much more should we all—without regard to rank or station—be in submission one to another.

In Hebrews 13:17 we see clearly the two sides of submission. No sooner are we commanded to obey and submit to our leaders than we are reminded that those very leaders labor under a sobering mandate: They must one day give an account. In Ephesians 6:1–9 we see Paul exhort fathers and masters to exercise their authority in a way that does not provoke those under their authority.

Even a verse like 1 Corinthians 11:3, in which we see a divinely ordered hierarchy, does not provide justification for the exercise of unqualified rulership as it has sometimes been interpreted. Paul says, here, that God is the head of Christ, Christ is the head of man and man is the head of the woman. This seems straightforward, but this verse is often taken out of context. It must be seen between two bookends. In 10:31, Paul anchors what he has said and what he is about to say with this injunction: "Do all to the glory of God" (NASB). He defines what that means practically in verse 32: "Give no offense either to Jews or to Greeks or to the church of God" (NASB). That means everybody!

Now go to the other bookend in 11:11–12, which says, "In the Lord, however, woman is not independent of man, nor is man independent of woman. For as woman came from man, so also man is born of woman. But everything comes from God." Paul seems confused here. It seems that he just described a hierarchy of relations in verse 3, placing the woman under the headship of the man. Now he seems to say that they are mutually dependent on each other.

How do we make sense of this? The same way we understood that the Father and the Son are co-equal in value although one can be subordinate to the other when it comes to their unique functions in their missions, such as redemption. The headship that a husband expresses to his wife (which seems to be the context of 1 Corinthians 11) is that which helps them accomplish their mutually desired purposes. Consider the way function and value interplay within the Trinity. The mission is mutually agreed to before any structure of subordination is engaged. This shows their equality of value. The Father did not decide to redeem and then impose His desires on the Son. The mission to save us was desired mutually by all three Persons in the Godhead. Because they equally desired it, they each had no problem fulfilling a function that created a chain of command, so to speak. So we see the Son *functionally* subordinated to the Father. It is a willing subordination, as Paul shows in Philippians 2:6–8.

Back to the Marriage Relationship

The same guidelines apply to a marriage. Let's say a husband and wife decide to renovate a room in their house. They come to the decision mutually (equality of value), then start working on the practicalities together. Part of the process of working out the practicalities is deciding what functions each must carry out. If the wife is better at interior design, she takes the lead functionally in choosing paint colors, and in that particular act the husband follows her lead. But then they have to decide which grade of paint they can afford. She wants a higher grade than their predetermined budget can handle. He is concerned with a decision that could place them under financial stress. He takes the lead in addressing this concern (hierarchy of function).

Some would say, "Well, he's the head; he should make the final call." But is that the right understanding of headship? If authority is "authoring," then fundamentally it is about creating a life-giving environment. Does the husband exercise his headship by making the decision? Or by creating a context in which they can mutually come to a decision? I suggest Paul would say the latter.

"What if the husband uses his position to make the decision?" Then that husband is not walking in true headship. The husband is to lead the process of problem solving, not make the decision unilaterally.

"But what if the wife is stubborn and won't discuss the issue reasonably?" Then she is not genuinely submitting to her husband's headship by creating an environment of honor.

The two sides of submission are seen clearly in the way the "authority relationship" is practically walked out. The "head" is called to create an environment of life, exercising rule only as it becomes necessary to preserve and nourish life (which does at times require a leader to exercise "tough love"). In our example, the husband creates an environment of life by patiently going over the numbers with his wife, or by seeking to see her point of view, or by offering alternatives to expensive paint that may be even better. The one "under" the head is called to create an environment of honor. In this case, the wife does that by listening to her husband's financial concerns without resistance or by affirming his efforts at finding a compromise. In so doing, the husband and wife mutually create an environment in which order and authority are the by-products of such "life" and "honor."

"But what if they still disagree?" The one primarily responsible to nurture an environment of life makes the final decision, based on the previously agreed-to purpose of renovating the room. In this case, the wife sees the need to yield to her husband as fulfilling her more important desire for a remodeled room.

Even here, however, God has a blessing for the one who must ultimately yield: the blessing of His presence. For when any of us—in this case, the wife—find ourselves in the minority position, and our desires are not realized, we are powerless in that particular situation. But God says that He is close to the powerless (see Psalms 33:18–22; 34:18; 1 Corinthians 1:26–27). So whenever you and I feel that we have to submit in a particular situation, we can rejoice! God will compensate for that with His very presence—as long as we do not become resentful and block His expressions of love to us.

13

Signs of an Authority Problem

There are two kinds of people: those who say to God, "Thy will be done," and those to whom God says, "All right, then, have it your way."

C. S. Lewis

The story of Miriam and Aaron's rebellion against Moses, recorded in Numbers 12, is one of Scripture's most descriptive accounts of the consequences of insubordination toward authority. Miriam and Aaron had an "authority problem" with Moses. In reading their story, we may find ourselves in them. Their attitudes and reactions may seem uncomfortably familiar as we recall moments in which *we* resisted authority.

What makes this story so significant (after all, there are a number of instances of rebellion in Scripture) is the closeness of the relationship Miriam and Moses surely enjoyed. She had been given the preeminent prophetic place under Moses. For a woman to be honored in that way in that culture was profound. Moreover, Miriam and Moses would have enjoyed a familial communion known only to siblings. So her rebellion here flares not from any supposed sense of dishonor or neglect. She is simply offended. Her response to Moses is pure, "unqualified" rebellion, and that is why this story is so important to understand. Her responses give us a clue as to what unbridled rebellion looks like even in its incipient stage. How can we tell when we have a problem submitting to legitimate authority, and what does this story teach us?

Tensions had been developing between Miriam and Moses for a while. The flash point that ignited Miriam's outburst was Moses' marriage to a Cushite woman. Yet this was but a cover for the real irritant lurking in her heart, a burr in her soul that we can detect in her antagonistic question: "Has the LORD spoken only through Moses? . . . Hasn't he also spoken through us?" (Numbers 12:2). Since Miriam bore the brunt of God's displeasure, it is reasonable to assume that she was the instigator of this squabble. At issue was Miriam's sense of entitlement. She was not just a prophetess; she was *the* prophetess of Israel. She was also Moses' older sister who deserved a certain amount of respect, and she was clearly peeved at what she regarded as Moses' claim of primacy.

The Pathway of Offense

How did these siblings, who had endured so much together, allow petty insecurities to trigger such a fractious quarrel? To understand how they got here, we have to go back a few weeks. The book of Numbers picks up Israel's story when the people were about to depart from Mount Sinai. From slavery in Egypt God had led them to the base of this mountain, and it was here that the Law had just been given. But something happened at this mountain that was to define Israel's relationship to the Lord from then on. Exodus 20 records the incident. Before Moses ascended Sinai, the people approached him with a sense of dread and foreboding. They were not quite sure what to make of this mountain exploding before them in fire and thunder, but they were quite sure they did not want to get close to a God like this.

And so they complained to Moses, saying in essence, "Do not have God speak to us or we will die. You be the mediator between us and God." Sadly, they had totally misconstrued what God was doing. Moses understood it and desperately tried to help the people understand. "Don't you see what God is doing?" Moses pleaded. "He is trying to keep you from sinning." Moses knew that God's pyrotechnics grandly expressed His desire for intimacy with His people. The Lord was revealing Himself in this way so that they would be far more impressed with His power than with the giants they were going to face in Canaan. But they resisted. Having seen the Red Sea part, Pharaoh humbled, Egypt's firstborn lying dead throughout the land and water flow out of a rock—after all this, they resisted.

The Reluctance to Worship

Resistance to authority does not begin with an act of defiance toward a leader or revolt against a government. It does not initially manifest in divisive attitudes. It does not even start with running stop signs here and there or displaying sarcastic bumper stickers aimed at the President. What Israel's story tells us is that *rebellion begins with a refusal to embrace intimacy with God*. Rebellion begins with a stiff neck—a reluctance to bend when prompted to worship. It can be as subtle as that. A simple refusal to lift one's hands in praise because it does not feel comfortable or to our liking. Or the unwillingness to turn the television off and reflect on the Lord's goodness when prompted to do so. It is the same "We don't want a God like that" attitude expressed thousands of years ago. In short, one of the first signs that we have an authority problem is an imperceptible but very real hardening of the heart when God summons us to greater intimacy with Himself.

This is one of the reasons why worship is so absolutely central. Worship, I suggest, is the key to experiencing the Lordship of Christ in our lives. For as Psalm 22:3 exhorts, the Lord's rulership is expressed and experienced when we worship.

When God told Moses to demand Pharaoh to let His people go, it was for this reason: that they would be given an opportunity to worship Him (see Exodus 5:1). This moment at Sinai was all about worship. It was about setting into Israel's culture the cornerstone of their foundation as a people, the supreme attitude that would enable them to walk faithfully under His law.

Anytime we resist God's command to worship, we start down a road of ultimate rebellion. The unwillingness to be pliable and bendable to the will of the Lord at this point is often the tip-off that we have allowed rebellion to take seed in our hearts.

Impatience with God's Order and Design

Throughout the opening chapters of Numbers we find Moses being given detailed instructions as to how Israel was to be organized. The setting apart of the Levites, the order in which the tribes were to march, the arrangement of the various tribes when they encamped around the tabernacle. There is nothing random here—only design, detailed design. When one hears Miriam, and later Korah, complain that Moses was setting himself up as God's primary spokesman, one can detect a certain impatience with order. And this can be another sign that we have an authority problem. Are we impatient and easily frustrated with protocols and procedures? I am not talking about the kind of mindset that is so "by the book" that it suffocates spontaneity and joy; I am simply talking about the willingness to align to God's patterns of doing things—what the Bible calls His *ways*.

Yes, vibrant Christianity is a matter of the inner life, and we can find ourselves too focused on the outward trappings of religion and not the all-important habits of the heart. God is not just the God of the grand sweep, however, but also the Steward of the smallest detail. He is the Master of the universe who, in the Person of Christ, yields to the protocols of John's baptism to fulfill all righteousness. He is the Lord who, at the moment history is split at His glorious rising, takes the time to fold His grave clothes.

If He were a factory worker, He would diligently fill out His time card. If He were doing His taxes, He would take care to be accurate. He would not chafe at the day's inconvenient demands, nor balk at life's sometimes necessary but needling red tape. He would still fold the grave clothes. Such an attitude shows a willingness to bend to systems and structures.

Unwillingness to Share Authority

In Numbers 11, as God distributes His Spirit to the seventy elders, we see Moses' willingness to share authority. Moses' response was not the clutching posture of one whose turf was threatened, but rather the magnanimity of a heart that is eager to share authority.

During an intense phase of the Civil War, General Grant—who had known nothing but a stunning succession of victories—found himself mired in the Siege of Petersburg. His army had made very little progress for several months. The juggernaut he was used to commanding now looked impotent. Grant's "failures" were the buzz of the politicos in Washington. At this same time, his good friend General Sherman appeared invincible, his campaign in the South an unqualified success. So, naturally, the talk percolated that Sherman should replace Grant as lieutenant general of the Union Army.

When Sherman heard of this, he wrote to Grant, "I have written to stop it. I would rather have you in command than anyone else." One would think Grant would dig his heels in, protecting his position. But Grant's response shows the kind of magnanimity of heart that marks one who understands authority: "No one would be more pleased with your advancement than I; and if you should be placed in my position, and I put your subordinate . . . I would support you as you have supported me."

A leader who is reticent to share authority actually shows that he or she has an authority problem, because an unwillingness to share authority when we are leaders reveals a disposition that is equally unwilling to let a leader lead when we are followers.

Listening to the Discontented

After three days of traveling from Mount Sinai, the Lord's presence came to rest (see Numbers 10:33). No sooner had the people set up camp than they began to complain that they had no food. What is revealing about this part of the story is found in Numbers 11:4: "The rabble with them began to crave other food, and again the Israelites started wailing and said, 'If only we had meat to eat!' " It seems that it was not the whole camp of Israel who complained, initially, but a fringe group simply identified as the "rabble," most likely Egyptians who had cast their lots with Israel.

There is a rabble in every church. There always seems to be a small faction in any Christian group whose expertise seems to be torpedoing the group's purpose. They excel in pointing out the negative, and most often target those in leadership. They are not antagonistic, necessarily; they just grumble. Unfortunately, this faction often has a negative impact on the rest of the congregation. Yet they sometimes serve a purpose, though most of us would not mind if they planted themselves elsewhere.

What they do, when they criticize or complain, is expose the roots of offense in the rest of us. When we listen to them and entertain their gripes, turning their negative comments over in our mind, it shows that there is something in our hearts to which their grumbling can "Velcro." Their grumbling finds an echo in us. Why? Because there is a place somewhere in our hearts where we are sensitive toward authority. Perhaps we have been hurt, maybe overlooked by a supervisor—whatever the reason, we have an offense. Because we have an offense toward authority, the rabble's murmuring gives us a chance to vent our own frustration toward leadership. We may even be okay with the particular authority we are presently under but harbor an imperceptible resentment toward another authority, which we do not even recognize—until we catch ourselves listening to the discontent of others. If we find ourselves bending an ear to such talk, it shows that we have an authority problem.

A "Never Enough" Attitude

The reason for the Israelites' discontent was their dissatisfaction with God's provision of food. They became restless with the one hundred and one ways to serve manna. They wanted meat, so God gave it to them in spades—a sea of quail in which their appetite went ballistic. They hounded God, then hoarded His provision. Interesting how an attitude of ingratitude goes hand in hand with a "spirit of grab." Possessive, stingy, ungenerous. These are words that describe a clutching person, the one who "never has enough."

And such attitudes betray an authority problem. They groused about what their "Authority"—God—had done for them. Ingratitude is basically an accusation against our ultimate authority, God. Ingratitude becomes habitual complaining, and that shapes us to be Scrooges. We always want more and experience inner conniptions when asked to share. In fact, the "never enough" attitude can be seen in the rampant materialism in American culture. Ours is a culture marked, to a great degree, by needing the bigger and the better. Does our materialism go hand in hand with our antagonism toward authority? I think there is a connection between an ever-addicting consumerism and ever-increasing rebellion.

Envy of Someone Else's Opportunity or Position

All of this is background to the story of Miriam and Aaron's opposition to Moses. It is interesting that in both Miriam's, and later Korah's, rebellion the root irritant is a perceived inequality that bred within each an envy of Moses' place before God. The idea that God places people over people stirred unease then and it stirs unease now. Part of the reason is that we often continue to confuse equality of value with equality of function. Since we believe we are all equally valuable, we can tend to feel entitled to the same functions in the Body of Christ, or at least the same status on the pecking order.

There are two consequences when we feel so entitled. The first is that demanding equality actually erodes our sense of uniqueness, which is one of the keys to feeling valuable and significant in the first place. We often forget that there are spiritual graces associated with each and every particular role, reserved just for that particular function. And when we pine for another's place, skills or position, we shut ourselves off from one of the most nourishing sources of personal significance.

The second consequence is that our demand for equality undermines the process of developing inner authority—for it is when we accept a place under someone else with grace that we give God a chance to promote us. And it is as we allow *God* to promote us that we cultivate an inner sense of confidence that buds when we know we are not advertising ourselves or manipulating to get our way. John the Baptist was "a man sent from God" (John 1:6, NASB). When God promotes us, we can walk in genuine confidence. Joseph is another biblical hero who knew the painful yet exquisitely satisfying process of being promoted by the Lord (see Psalm 105:16–22).

So, not only does our demand for equality blur the distinctions of our own uniqueness, but it actually undermines our chance of becoming whole by letting the Lord promote us to ever-increasing levels of responsibility and authority. The process of promotion is a wonderful thing, because it is the process in which honoring can occur. And remember, God will always make a way for us. There is no human being who can keep you from your God-given purpose and destiny. Even if God has to remove you from a structure that does not recognize God's promotion of you, He can do it. But we have to let *Him* do it, rather than taking the matter into our own hands.

Threatened by Another's Success

Not only can we become envious of a leader under whom we are assigned to function, we can feel threatened as well. And the sense of threat cuts both ways: either on the part of the one assigned to be under another's leadership or on the part of a leader nervous about a subordinate's growing influence or ability. This sense of threat can quickly turn to anger, which can actually be an expression of anger toward God. Before this family tiff, Israel's rebelliousness had been directed toward God. But now—in the persons of Miriam and Aaron—it is directed toward Moses' leadership.

We have seen, when God distributed His Spirit to the seventy elders in Numbers 11, Moses' willingness to share authority. And that is what makes Miriam's rebellion so disconcerting. Moses had already demonstrated that he was humble enough to allow the anointing to be shared among his peers, so why would she feel threatened? Was Miriam rebellious because she was actually threatened by other prophetically gifted people? Because God had raised up seventy others who had the potential to prophecy? Because her treasured place of esteem was in jeopardy? That possibility looms large in this story.

The feeling of being threatened when others are promoted is a sign that we have an authority problem. Notice that Miriam grasps for spiritual equality here: "I am as anointed as you." It is not that this is untrue, for as we have stated, we are equal. But we cannot grasp for it, any more than the Master did not grasp for it—for He considered equality with God as something He did not have to insist on (see Philippians 2:5–7).

Miriam did not express her rebellion directly, but looked for a legitimate excuse to vent her rebellion, which as we have seen was Moses' questionable marriage to a Cushite woman. (Some scholars suggest this was not a breach of cultural protocols or of God's command, since He had commanded only that the Israelites could not marry a Canaanite.)

A sure sign that we have an authority problem is this sense of threat that engenders in us a heart that is easily offended. Miriam was offended at both Moses' exaltation and the expanded number of Spirit-inspired leaders. Now she had to find some legitimate reason for her offense so that she could vent her rebellion.

Seeking to Legitimize Our Offense

Offense will seek legitimacy. One of the telltale signs of an offended spirit is the compulsion to keep score, to rack up wrongs and tally another's shortcomings. The need to stack the evidence against someone is a subtle sign that we are offended somewhere and that we are being emotionally dominated by an inner push to justify our resentment. We look for an issue that seems reasonable to us and to those around us, so that the offense is seen as an expression of justice or the understandable airing of a grievance.

I know of one congregation that suffered grave consequences because of a deacon who ended up splitting the church. Years before he became a deacon, his life became miserable. His family was a wreck, his job was in jeopardy. One night he was trying to pray but was feeling very resentful about his circumstances. While he was praying—as he tells it—an angel visited him and told him that he needed to go to a certain church and set that church in order. The seeds of betrayal were sown in his heart even then, and years later when he became a deacon he proceeded to "set that church in order"—which led him to lead a group of people against the pastor.

What is disturbing about this story is that the root of his act of betrayal lay in his offense toward the Lord for allowing his life to become what it had become. His offense toward God led him to seek grounds for accusing another. His drive to set the church in order was his way of legitimizing his offense.

Grasping for Recognition

Miriam's need to justify her offense goes hand in hand with her itch to be recognized—and this is another sign of an authority problem. Whenever we find ourselves perturbed that we have been overlooked, or that our gifts have not been recognized, we need to take note. For often that little bent shows we have a "pre-condition" toward being easily offended. Moses displays the right heart here. He was not possessive about his gift. His desire was that "all God's people prophesy."

Unwilling to Follow When Unsure of a Leader's Direction

Finding ourselves uncertain about the direction a leader or group of leaders is taking presents us with one of the most challenging tests of submission. And that uncertainty can become a disagreement. The disagreement itself is not wrong, but what we do with it can be when questioning becomes criticizing.

Following a leader when uncertain of his or her direction is a tough assignment. All of us have felt chagrined at times when we have blindly followed a leader, only to find ourselves disillusioned or perhaps even abused. Because there is such distrust in many toward leadership, the imperative to follow can prompt understandable resistance. Nevertheless, there is a truth here that we cannot ignore. There are times when we will be called to engage with a leader even when we are not quite sure that where he is headed is right.

It needs to be stated flatly, of course, that issues of morality, heresy and ethics are not here in contest. The Bible gives no authorization for any to follow a leader into sin or to violate obvious scriptural standards. I am referring more to those times when a leader summons us to a task of which we are just not certain. Perhaps our pastor is advocating a building program, and we wonder if that is the best use of the church's money. Or a wife chooses to submit to her husband regarding their vacation destination, even though she wonders if it is the best use of time.

Miriam did not simply question Moses; she criticized him. Questioning leadership is not wrong; dialoguing with leaders is not wrong. But openly criticizing a leader is.

Of course, most of us do not blatantly criticize. We have more subtle ways of manipulating leaders. Even the most spiritually sensitive can conceal low-grade resistance toward authority and be unaware of it. During Elijah's prophetic ministry in Israel, he founded schools of the prophets. The day Elijah was to be taken to heaven, the Lord revealed this fact to many of the prophets. They knew Elijah was going to be translated to glory, because they kept telling Elisha. But after Elijah was taken up in a whirlwind, these same prophets, reluctant to let go of the past, urged Elisha to let them go look for him. Elisha knew this to be misguided, and told them so. But this passage in 2 Kings 2 says that these prophets kept dinging him to the point that he was made to feel ashamed. They persisted to the point of manipulating Elisha by shaming him.

This reveals a definite authority problem. When we try to get our way—even if going about it sweetly—and have a hard time taking no for an answer, we may have an authority problem. Criticism is not just the venting of verbal assault; it may be the tack of wearing down an authority figure by coming at him from several angles until he is worn down.

And remember, humility goes both ways. The humble leader will do all he can to reach consensus, explain his actions, allow questions from his followers. He will not feel threatened by those who question his leadership. By the same token, humility is expressed in followers who, having asked their questions and yet without satisfactory answers, still follow their leaders.

Pleasing People Rather Than Pleasing God

Miriam is not the only one at fault here, although she seems to receive the brunt of the correction. Aaron, too, exhibits an authority problem, but in a different way. He, as we know, was a people pleaser from way back, his colors clearly revealed when he caved in to the crowd in the golden calf incident (see Exodus 32). He was more interested in what people thought of him than he was in pleasing God. So when Miriam baits him with her offense, he quickly sides with her.

This "playing both sides against the middle" trait becomes especially destructive in the heat of controversy. If we are functioning in a line of authority under a supervisor and that supervisor is criticized, we will tend to empathize with the discontented instead of maintaining a righteous loyalty toward our superior. And the disloyalty is manifest not so much in attacking the leader; instead, we simply say nothing. That is as destructive as if we were intentionally to take sides. Even if the leader is wrong, we should first seek to cover his or her weaknesses—something that Ham did not do for his father, Noah (see Genesis 9:20–23)—and then go to that leader privately.

More Passionate about the Spiritual Gifts Than the Spiritual Giver

There is another, more subtle, sign of an authority problem. Miriam's objection—"Doesn't God speak to us as well?"— reveals that she was preoccupied with her spiritual gifts more than her passion for God. John Calvin said of this passage that Miriam and Aaron extolled the gift of revelation and prophecy more than the author who gave the gifts, who is the Lord!

Being more passionate about spiritual gifts than the spiritual Giver can indicate that we have the seeds of self-absorption within us. If we are self-focused we are apt to resist authority, because we will tend to view authority as a barrier to our personal—and often hidden—agenda.

Defensive Attitudes

Moses does not defend himself. One who responds well to authority will be slow to speak in the face of criticism.

He so understands that authority is given by God that he will not grasp it even when his own position is threatened. Conversely, one who does not respond well to authority is quick to defend himself. In my life, the quickness by which I defend myself shows that I am quick to criticize others in authority.

Then you might ask, "Why didn't Paul stay silent when his authority was questioned?" First, Paul asserted his authority only when the Gospel was at stake, not to keep his following. Second, he did it only when he was forced into it—and then he defended himself by presenting himself as a "fool" (see 2 Corinthians 10–13)!

A leader who is quick to defend himself shows that he may secretly believe that possessing authority is merely a transactional arrangement between humans and not a delegated privilege from God—and then naturally will feel that people have the right to criticize. If a leader really understands that authority is delegated from God, he will not be quick to criticize, especially those under his care.

A Sobering Caveat

There seems to be a domino effect in this story as we see Miriam's insubordination play out. She and Aaron were the leaders closest to Moses. And it appears that their rebellion opened the door of rebellion to the rest of the nation. The prophetess and the priest—family members at that—were the ones who rebelled. Little wonder that in the following chapter we find the next tier of leadership reacting against Moses.

There is a principle here: Sin in leadership uncovers those who are directly under our sphere of leadership. The specific sins of the leader often become the snares of those under his leadership. This does not mean that they have to give in to the temptation—in this case, unlawfully criticizing leadership—but it does mean that they become vulnerable to temptations toward the sins to which their leaders open the door. For example, when a pastor commits adultery, I suggest this alters the spiritual climate and gives the enemy occasion to intensify his temptation of the flock in that specific area.

The Compulsion to Demand Equality

As we saw earlier, the Israelites' complaints became the catalyst for the creation of an eldership council (see Numbers 11). Moses gladly agreed with God's purpose to distribute His Spirit upon seventy tribal heads, showing once again his unselfish, "palms-up" posture toward his own authority. But it is striking that, in contrast, some high-ranking community leaders were later influenced by Korah to rise up against Moses in the name of "equality and justice," as we see in Numbers 16. Their anointing and authority became a pretext for rebellion! New privileges can often spawn old pride—pride that has been there all along, perhaps, but has not had a trigger point of exposure until new levels of position and authority are given.

The Korah story is unsettling because the reason stated for the rebellion was based in a perceived justice issue. What was stuck in Korah's craw was the fact that Moses' primacy seemed to overshadow the privileges of the rest of the people. Korah's rebellion was masked by sentiments of equanimity. He comes off as a defender of the little guy, a Frank Capra sort, a muckraker who stands for truth and justice. Of course we need men and women of conscience who expose injustice. But we must be ever vigilant toward our own heart, so that our own zeal for justice is not rooted in our own offense.

14

Confronting Authority with Correction

> To punish me for my contempt for authority, fate made me an authority myself.
>
> Albert Einstein

Submission to authority is not always as black and white as we would like. For what happens when an authority figure is clearly wrong? How are we to respond when a leader compromises clear biblical standards, or harms others by his controlling behaviors? How do we navigate between right compliance with a leader's direction, even when we may be unsure of it, and the necessity of confronting that leader when he is in error? Those in authority are human, after all, and will make mistakes. But it is difficult to know when and how to approach them. How do we express concern to a leader without becoming accusing? Some feel duty-bound to correct a leader's every error; others are timid to say anything at any time for fear of "touching the Lord's anointed." There are many biblical heroes who were faced with just such a challenge, and there is much wisdom we can learn from them.

When Asked to Do Something Questionable

When it comes to walking the tightrope between compliance and confrontation, the young Daniel is a model for all of us, especially youth. For it was as a young teenager that he was carted off to Babylon—to a completely foreign culture bereft of family and familiar surroundings. Lauded for his physical appearance and intellectual aptitude, he was pressed into the king's service and enlisted in a training regimen designed to make good pagans of young lads. He was commanded to eat a daily ration of food and wine from the king's table. The only problem was that the king's table was not kosher. To have obeyed the authority in this case would have meant violating God's law.

Thus, Daniel found himself in a dilemma. He could have pulled his self-righteous robes around him and simply protested. A hunger strike maybe. But rather than take a combative posture, Daniel offered his immediate supervisor—the guard assigned to him—a plan that would allow Daniel to obey God's higher law awhile longer and let the guard protect his position. "Test me and my friends for ten days," Daniel suggested, "and let us eat only vegetables and drink only water. Then at the end of ten days evaluate us."

At the end of the ten days, Daniel and his friends looked healthier and better nourished than any of the young men who feasted on the royal diet.

Daniel's example gives us some excellent wisdom points.

Wisdom Point #1: *Appeal before you confront.*

When confronting an authority figure, pose your confrontation as an invitation to dialogue rather than as a statement of your opinion—or worse yet, as an accusation.

Daniel did not deride the king's choice of food, nor did he frame the choice between his diet and the king's as one in which his was superior over the other. Instead, Daniel entreated the guard, and did not force the guard into a position in which he had to prove himself. By posing the correction as a question rather than an accusation, Daniel actually assumed the risk of the confrontation. In doing so, he put himself, as the subordinate, in a learning posture. This invites the authority figure to consider the question rather than have to respond to an accusation or defend his position.

For example, a subordinate might say to a superior, "I am sensing something here, and I want you to help me see if what I am sensing is right." Or when feeling uneasy about a decision his superior is about to make, he might ask, "Is it possible that you may not have the full picture of what you are about to do?"

Let's say your supervisor becomes testy in a committee meeting. Knowing that his testiness was uncalled for and that his momentary demanding demeanor hurt someone else in the group, you might find an appropriate, private moment to say to him, "I know you have been carrying an awfully big load recently, and we are so appreciative of that fact. But I couldn't help but sense that you feel under the gun for some reason. Is there a way I can help? I can appreciate your reasons for responding in the way you did. But have you considered how your responses have affected other people?"

This leads to a second wisdom point:

Wisdom Point #2: *Look for something that you can affirm.*

In most confrontation scenarios there is some aspect of the issue about which you can be positive. We should be especially sensitive to this when confronting a leader. Be willing to express this early in the dialogue. If there is nothing positive, at least be careful not to camp on *all* the negatives. In Daniel's case, he did not resist the king's schooling entirely, though there were certainly other pagan influences with which he had to contend. He just confronted one particular issue.

Recently my fourteen-year-old daughter, Caleigh, who is budding into a terrific pianist, was practicing one of her more demanding pieces. As I listened, enraptured, she suddenly began to pound the ivories mercilessly. Now, our piano is not just any piano. It is an antique 1923 Chickering baby grand. I rushed into the room and duly rebuked her for abusing such a treasure.

Caleigh's response was quick: "Well, you pound on the piano as hard as I do."

No sooner had the words left her mouth than she at once sweetened up. She knew that she had just confronted her father with a right issue in a wrong way. So she quickly adjusted course and said with a smile, "Well, I *have* heard you play the piano just as hard as me. But you're the father, so it's okay for you to do that."

Now of course it is *not* okay for me to do that. Caleigh was right, and I was being unjust. I was expecting her to behave in a way that I had not been willing to do. I quickly told her that just because I was the dad did not give me license to break the rules and act unjustly. Nevertheless, her follow-up response did indicate to me that she was getting a good grasp on this issue of authority—for she affirmed my place as her father but still was able to slip the corrective in.

Daniel showed amazing discretion. He approached the guard privately and did not make a public spectacle of his protest. This shows that he knew how to handle sensitive information. To be a person of discretion means to have the ability to handle confidences well. Daniel did not tell the king to change his policy; he simply invited his superiors to witness the change in himself. To be a person of discretion means knowing how to use the information you have wisely. It is knowing when to be silent. It is the art of being as wise as a serpent and as harmless as a dove.

All this shows that Daniel had developed a prior track record of discretion.

Wisdom Point #3: *Be wary of confronting an authority if you have not developed discretion.*

When we are confronting an authority figure, sometimes our need to assert an opinion at the very outset of the encounter shows that we may be in an insecure position—possibly not knowing all the facts, possibly feeling threatened. And this takes us to a fourth principle.

Wisdom Point #4: *Do not confront an authority figure if you are feeling insecure; wait for the peace of the Spirit.*

As long as you feel anxious, hold off on appealing to or confronting one in authority. What may happen, otherwise, is that the person's responses—based simply on the sheer weight of his or her position of authority—will intimidate you. This will only intensify your insecurity, complicating further dialogue.

Make sure you know all the facts and have thought through all the possible reasons why an authority figure may have responded or acted in the way he or she did. Often we see a leader through only one lens. We may, for example, see a leader become impatient or easily offended. But have we taken the time to ask the Lord how He sees that leader?

Many years ago my Bible college president, Dick Foth, said that his number one prayer, when it came to his own life, was "Lord, give me perspective." Someone who modeled that well was Abigail.

When a Leader Is About to Do Wrong

Abigail's story, found in 1 Samuel 25, is even more intriguing than Daniel's, because she had to confront an authority figure quickly and decisively before that authority figure—David, Israel's soon-to-be king—committed murder! Here is the background: Abigail's husband, Nabal, was a wealthy landowner with considerable livestock. On one occasion his shepherds were in David's neck of the woods. David treated them hospitably and protected them from harm. Now David was in need, so he requested that Nabal supply his men with provisions. But Nabal was a churlish man with a stingy spirit. He refused them hospitality, and, in doing so, incensed David. So angry was David that he decided to take Nabal out—permanently.

Abigail got wind of David's reaction and knew she had to make a snap judgment. She realized she had to confront David, but she also knew that to confront a man of David's strength and stature was to invite his ire on her own head. So she prepared some hors d'oeuvres and sent them ahead with her servants. She followed close behind, and when she met David she sought to mollify his wrath by honoring him and speaking graciously to him.

Her example was a stunning display of diplomatic grace. And one of the keys to her wise approach was that she assumed the responsibility for her husband's foolishness ("On me alone, my lord, be the blame," verse 24, NASB). By so doing she was conveying to the leader that she was not one to shirk guilt, but was willing to be the scapegoat in order to help the leader—in this case David—save face.

Wisdom Point #5: *When confronting a leader, first acknowledge where you may be wrong in the situation.*

This takes the accusation out of the confrontation.

One wonders how Abigail could respond with such graciousness so quickly in the heat of the moment. I think it was because she was already in the habit of ruling her own heart. She had learned the art of controlling her emotions—not suppressing her emotions, but controlling them. And this brings us to another principle we learn from Abigail.

Wisdom Point #6: *Be slow to confront authority if you, yourself, have not been ruling your own heart.*

If you are given to sins of the tongue—expressing a critical spirit or gossiping—then you have disqualified yourself from being able to confront authority.

The difference between suppressing an emotion and controlling an emotion is that in suppressing an emotion we deny it. We bury it. We do not confront its reality. When anger flares or fear taunts, we look the other way. To control one's emotion is to acknowledge the reality of it, to face it even if painful, but then to refuse to let it dictate our actions.

To control one's emotions is to turn the emotion into something constructive. For example, the emotion of anger can be channeled to produce in us a problem-solving attitude—if we do not let it rule us. How? Well, anger has the power to focus us. If we just seethe within, we are letting anger rule us. But if we turn our anger away from the offending person and redirect it toward the problem, then we may find ourselves better focused on creating strategies to relieve the inner stress that person's actions or attitudes are causing us.

Abigail stayed attuned to the Holy Spirit. She ruled her spirit. She had learned to overcome her emotions. She was able, therefore, to offer wisdom to an influential person at the right moment. She was able to respond immediately and seize her opportunity. Had she been wallowing in her circumstances, despondent over an unfulfilling marriage and allowing negative emotions to rule her, she never would have been in a position to recognize her opportunity when it came.

Abigail's story has some timely insights for women. What happens when a woman finds herself in a structure that is confining? Abigail probably endured some of the most confining circumstances of any woman in the Old Testament. She lived in obscurity, caught in a dead-end marriage to a surly husband. Talk about going nowhere! But the Lord had destined her to be a queen, the wife of one of the greatest kings who has ever lived. God fashioned her for this even in her mother's womb.

So how does a person like Abigail move from her dead-end situation to becoming the wife of a king?

Recently I came across the story of a woman who was struggling in her local church over the fact that in that particular culture there were few opportunities given to women to minister. She could have been offended, but she chose to rule her spirit and maintain a stance of support and honor toward the leadership. Over the course of several months she continued to walk poised, smiling, always exhibiting a joyous attitude.

In due course the pastor found himself dealing with a particularly thorny counseling situation that was too much for him to handle. He realized that he needed input from another source. All at once he remembered that smiling face, the warm, gracious person he had seen again and again at services, and thought, *That woman is sharp. I need to talk to her.*

So he sought her advice. Even here, the woman had to walk sensitively and wisely in the situation. The opportunity had presented itself, but now she had a choice. She could either "seize" her opportunity, overpowering the pastor with a waterfall of information, or she could carefully offer input bit by bit and watch how the pastor responded. She prudently did the latter.

Once this woman was on the pastor's radar she was given more opportunities and responsibilities, because, like Abigail, she watched and knew how to manage wisely the opportunities given her. In other words, because she had learned how to keep her emotions in check she had developed discernment. She knew how—and how much—she should communicate to a leader when given the opportunity.

Wisdom Point #7: *If you have learned to rule your heart, you will be better prepared to walk in discernment.*

Discernment was a real key for Abigail, but that discernment was an outcome of the fact that she ruled her spirit continually. You do not just get discernment when the opportunity presents itself. Discernment is the overflow of a lifestyle of learning to rise above your circumstances.

It is one thing to recognize your opportunity. It is another to know how to handle that opportunity wisely. Discernment is not only the ability to understand a situation; it is wisdom to manage the conflict.

Back to the critical moment. When Abigail, hearing that Nabal had rejected David, sized up the situation, her initial response was to manage the conflict by meeting the most immediate need. In this case the immediate need was hunger; therefore, she prepared raisin cakes and refreshments to appease David's anger. When she realized that David was on the verge of making a disastrous decision, she looked for his most pressing need and addressed it.

Most of the time when we are admonishing an authority figure we will not be blessing him or her with raisin cakes.

But the principle of looking for the most pressing need—and often it is an emotional one—holds true. And this brings us to our next wisdom point.

Wisdom Point #8: *When confronting an authority figure, find out where he or she is needy and fill that need.*

Often the leader's need is for respect. So we can derive a quick corollary to the next wisdom point:

Wisdom Point #9: *Honor comes before honesty.*

If you feel that you need to be honest with your leader about something, then pave the way with honor so that he or she can be more receptive to your honest critique.

When a Leader Has Already Erred

Esther was another woman who showed extraordinary tact and courage when called to confront an authority figure—which, in her case, was the most powerful authority in the world. Not only that, but her circumstances were much more formidable. For she was not limited by mere church protocols or societal conventions. She was constrained by the very law of the land. Even as the queen, to go into the king's presence uninvited was to risk her life.

Esther's story is epic. The Persian king, taken with her beauty, chose her to be his queen, but later was hoodwinked into passing a law dooming her people, the Jews, to certain death. She was thus confronted with the supreme justice issue: obey man's law or obey God's law. The way she dealt with this dilemma is illuminating for us who find ourselves caught between this rock and hard place, wanting to be properly submissive to authority on the one hand but faithful to God on the other—when that authority is contravening His standards.

Esther actually had two authorities. She was, of course, under the governmental and marital authority of the king. But God provided her with an influencing authority, her cousin Mordecai. Mordecai was able to give her wisdom: ways to navigate the situation that enabled her to retain her integrity, did not jeopardize her life prematurely and kept her honoring her husband the king all at the same time.

Wisdom Point #10: *When under an authority whom you know is making wrong decisions, look for someone who can give you wise counsel.*

If you find yourself in a straightjacket like Esther was, look for a Mordecai—an influencing authority who can help you know

- how to express honor toward the authority without compromising God's Word;
- when to push forward with your concerns;
- when to hold back;
- and when to lay your life on the line.

In Esther's case there was no avoiding the daunting reality that she was going to have to confront her husband the king. But when she did, she did so in a way that did not threaten him. She risked rejection, seeking not to put the king on the defensive. She stood up for her principles, but guarded his back.

This is what Paul the apostle did when he spoke out against the hypocrisy of the Jewish elders in Acts 23:3. When he was summarily rebuked, he did not react defensively. Instead, he guarded their backs by quickly looking for a way to justify their rebuke and enable them to save face (see verses 4–5). From this we glean another wisdom point.

Wisdom Point #11: *When you admonish an authority figure and he defends himself—and even refutes you harshly—build an emotional bridge to him by affirming his rebuke in some way.*

No doubt this is a tall order. Rebukes sting. Most of us react so instinctively, with barbed comebacks or hasty retreats, that we never really consider the possibility of building a bridge. Yet if we can somehow treat that moment heroically . . . somehow see ourselves as "saving" the authority figure by taking his side if only for a moment, looking for ways to at least partially validate his response—even if you feel it is unjust—perhaps it can open him to dialogue. And you will be able to make your point. Interestingly, to the extent that my reaction to rebuke is rejection, to that degree it may reveal whether my concern is simply to communicate truth—or to state my opinion.

Every so often we may find ourselves having to defy rules that are clearly morally wrong. Esther had to break the law— the law that said you could not go into the king's presence uninvited—in order to do what was right. But notice that when she did so she jeopardized no one but herself. When it comes to civil protest, the question we must ask ourselves is this: Are we using that protest to vent our anger? Is it an excuse for us to "get even" with an authority structure with whom we have an offense?

Esther did not defy the king's edict against her own people at this point. She chose to break a law that jeopardized only herself. And when she did so, she did it with a steadfast resolve, because she knew her sense of timing—the result of her submission to the influencing authority of Mordecai—was right. When she went into the king's presence, she did so meekly and with humility. Like Daniel, she was a person of discretion. This quality had been cultivated by her pattern of listening to wise counsel. Because she was teachable, she developed good judgment.

When Esther did go into the king's presence, she was selective in what she said. She did not confront the issue all at once. First the king was pleased with her, then she simply requested another meeting (see Esther 5:1–4). She did not initially raise the issue of injustice, for she had judiciously planned to unwrap the issue bit by bit. This is a vital strategy to understand.

Wisdom Point #12: *Before confronting an authority, design a communication plan.*

Imagine yourself broaching the issue a piece at a time. Imagine how your authority may respond, and plan your response. By thinking this through you will ready yourself to delay parts of the confrontation, if necessary. Let's say you find yourself needing to tell your supervisor that he has done something seriously wrong. See yourself meeting with him two or three times, and think of how you will enlighten him patiently stage by stage. In this way you will be able to measure his response and thus know how far you may be able to go.

One of the reasons, I suggest, that Esther could approach the king with such grace is that she did not treat him as if he was automatically wrong (despite what she may have thought to the contrary). She did not treat him as if he was shortsighted or narrow. Nothing in her demeanor or body language conveyed an attitude of faultfinding in her initial posture toward the king. When she confronted him she did not assume that he—the governmental authority under which she was operating—was wrong.

This leads to another principle we derive from Esther.

Wisdom Point #13: *When confronting an authority, assume his innocence as much you can.*

Maybe you cannot assume his innocence if his actions have been blatantly wrong. But at least you can give his motives the benefit of the doubt until proven otherwise.

This principle is imperative for intercessors and the more prophetically inclined. Those who have an unusual commitment to pray or who carry a keen sensitivity to the prompting of the Holy Spirit (those we may call "prophetic" in orientation) often tie their sense of personal worth to their personal revelations from God. When what they feel from God is a corrective to the authority under which God has placed them, the risks can be high. What they are putting on the table is their ability to hear God. Should that be challenged by the authority figure, it can be emotionally devastating because it goes to the very root of their identity and their sense of value before the Lord. Assuming that a leader has acted in good faith (even if that later proves to be wrong) is a prudent stance for us as intercessors to take, because it lessens the possibility of being unnecessarily rejected and thus buffers the risk of losing our confidence to hear God.

There is another angle to this that those influencing others—the Mordecais—need to remember. If the influencing authority is acting with integrity, he will not seek to sow seeds of distrust in those he is influencing toward their governmental or structural authority.

I recall talking to a friend of mine some years ago who found himself counseling two different couples from the same church who were thinking of leaving that particular church. In their estimation, that church had adopted practices that felt very authoritarian to them and they were no longer sure they wanted to be under that particular authority. My friend—another pastor in the city—could have easily taken the bait at that point, because he actually felt the same way about that church. But he knew that to use his influence to bend them away from the governmental authority that they were under would be sin. So he wisely steered a neutral course and just simply helped them to take their emotions out of the equation and look at things from a biblical point of view.

The specifics of his counsel are not important here. Suffice it to say that because this influencing authority was careful not to sow seeds of distrust in either couple, one couple went back to the church and submitted to that structure and is now flourishing wonderfully. The other couple felt called by God to withdraw from that authority and is equally flourishing. The point is that the influencer did not use his influence to undermine another's authority.

Esther knew that the governmental authority she was under was rightly operating in its sphere. Even though the structure was limiting, the king was not wholly wrong. He was being responsive to the legal authority within the structure he was governing. Had Mordecai subtly sown seeds into Esther causing her to despise the king, she would not have had the attitude of humility to navigate that whole situation. She may have tried to put on meekness in her audience with the king, for example, but it would not have come from her heart, and thus she would not have had authority. The only reason she had an inner authority to go against the law of the land was because she assumed that the governmental authority was to be respected.

When we understand the rights of a governmental authority—say, the "line authority" within a business—we will be more sensitive to the proper protocols of resolving conflict. If a person has an offense toward his manager, for example, he needs to go to that person *first* before going to his manager's supervisor. If it is a "leader to leader" issue, then the offended leader may go to his "up line" for processing but not for surrogate conflict resolution.

Let's say a senior manager has an issue with a peer-level person within his company. That manager may go to the other's immediate supervisor for advice and perspective, but should not try to goad that supervisor into resolving his conflict. (And of course the supervisor should maintain a stance of *impartiality*, not *neutrality*—which means that he affirms his *loyalty* to his subordinate while expressing understanding and a willingness to listen to the one bringing the complaint.)

When Dealing with a Character-Compromised Leader

Sometimes we find ourselves having to interrelate with a spiritual leader who clearly exhibits character flaws. That is where David found himself again and again with King Saul, and this is one of life's great crucibles of character.

When David had a chance to kill Saul, he left him alone, saying that he would not "touch the Lord's anointed." The issue of "touching the Lord's anointed" is one we need to de-lineate carefully, because at times it has been misunderstood. Leaders can unjustly use this concept to keep followers in check; followers can be overreluctant to raise valid issues for fear of incurring God's displeasure. So where do we land?

When given the opportunity to kill Saul, we can surmise that David wisely opted to pass it up for two reasons. First, David quite possibly discerned that Saul's character compro-mises were not immediately harming the people. Therefore he may have felt that to take Saul out may have done more harm to the people than leaving him to God's judgment. By responding in this way David was doing for Saul what Ham did not do for his own father, Noah. When Ham found Noah drunk and naked, he did not cover his disgrace but "shared his concerns" with his brothers—and was judged for it. Both Noah and Saul had compromised themselves and were clearly in the wrong. But in both instances their sin was not yet causing direct harm to those under their leadership. It is wiser in such cases to leave compromised leaders in God's hands, since He knows perfectly when and how to deal with them.

Wisdom Point #14: *Be slow to expose or criticize a character-compromised leader if you determine that his or her sin is not damaging others.*

David's second reason for not killing Saul may have been that he knew to do so would be to act out of revenge. The motive of revenge can be hard to detect, because it is at once rooted in both justice *and* personal offense. Revenge is at work in us anytime we seek justice to medicate our hurts.

From this we glean a final wisdom point.

Wisdom Point #15: *Do not expose or criticize a character-compromised leader if you sense that you are doing so out of your own offense.*

Conclusion

President Truman once said, "A government committed to the principle of silencing the voice of opposition has only one way to go . . . creating a country where everyone lives in fear." Those in positions of authority must create an environment in which people can safely register concerns. If those concerns relate to a leader's wrongs, then such a climate is all the more important. We as leaders must be approachable and teachable.

Those of us who find ourselves in a position in which we need to confront a leader should not forget that, as William Shakespeare admonished, we need to respond "wisely and slow. They stumble that run fast."

15

The Palms-Up Leader

A leader does not seek spiritual authority; a leader seeks to know God.

Robert Clinton

The single most important breakthrough of the second millennium of the Common Era was Johannes Gutenberg's development of movable type, which allowed books to be printed mechanically. Interestingly, the first two bestselling books that were printed after Gutenberg invented his press were Martin Luther's translation of the Bible into German and Niccolò Machiavelli's treatise on accruing power, *The Prince*.

It is intriguing that these two works—one, the account of a loving God who selflessly gives and serves; the other, a manual on how a leader seizes and maintains power—were released at nearly the same time. One can almost see the cosmic struggle in this: Luther championing the priesthood of all believers, Machiavelli unashamedly supporting the concentration of power in one individual. It was as if Satan—knowing how revolutionary getting Scripture into the hands of the masses was going to be, knowing that they would begin to learn principles of humility, love and servanthood firsthand—quickly fired a salvo of his own, the seduction of power, in an effort to countermand God's new offensive. This underscores just how basic this battle between power and humility is.

The question of who is in control may be the most pressing issue at hand. Is Christ really in control of His Church? He is, of course, in an ultimate sense, but does His Lordship define how we "do church" day by day? Leadership is often the pivotal arena in which the issue of Christ's control is played out, whether that is leading a family or superintending a denomination. Most spiritual leaders possess a genuine desire to please God and carry out their ministry with integrity. Yet the very nature of leadership carries with it subtle susceptibilities to pride. To exercise good leadership one needs to maintain some measure of quality control to ensure that intended objectives are realized. Appropriate supervision is an intrinsic aspect of leadership, but it is ever so easy for even the noblest of leaders to assume a permanent control that is not theirs.

Nietzsche said that the root issue of them all is the will to power. He may not have been far off. And for leaders power may be the ultimate seductress. If we are to align to godly authority, and if that is the key to personal freedom, then it is incumbent on us to discern how we as leaders can be noncontrolling in our leadership styles—the "palms-up" kind of leader.

Pictures of Leadership

There are many images that capture the effective leader: Inspirer. Empowerer. Visionary. Coach. Mentor. But what are those specific self-perceptions that affirm a leader's unique calling while at the same time reinforcing a servant mindset in the leader that avoids an unconstructive separation between "superiors" and "subordinates"? How should a leader perceive his or her authority in a way that acknowledges the importance of leadership without eroding the sense that all are of equal value? How can a leader *lead* without succumbing to the temptation to *control*?

Leaders as Gifts

First, we as leaders should see ourselves as "gifts" more than "generals." Ephesians 4:8, 11 says,

> "When he [Christ Jesus] ascended on high, he led captives in his train and gave gifts to men." . . . It was he who gave some to be apostles, some to be prophets, some to be evangelists, and some to be pastors and teachers.

Think of this! Jesus so loves His Church that He gives gifts to us, and He calls these "gifts" apostles, prophets, evangelists, pastors and teachers.

When I give a gift to my wife, Nancy—say a box of chocolates—my focus is not so much on the box of chocolates (the gift) as it is on my wife. I would be pretty shallow as a husband if I lavished my attention on the box of chocolates rather than my wife. And yet we tend to do that with leaders. Much attention, not altogether unwarranted, is focused on "leadership" in our culture. Because of this leaders can see themselves more as "generals," summoning the troops to battle and demanding allegiance.

This mindset is often reinforced by the management theorists of our day. Recently I heard a leadership development expert make this statement: "Everything hinges on leadership." This is a standard mantra in the political and business worlds, but is it a kingdom view? It is more accurate to say that everything hinges on *relationships*. A leader's leadership is in large part determined by his relationships with his or her followers.

As essential as leaders are, I would suggest that God's focus is not so much on the leader, the "gift," but on the recipient of the gift, His Church. Such a perspective does not minimize the role of a leader, but it should focus us on where a leader's place is in God's design. When I, as a leader, see myself as His gift to His people, it settles me both in my value to God—after all, boxes of chocolates are special—and in an accurate view of my place: I am but an expression of God's love to His Beloved.

Leaders as Shepherds Who Feed before They Lead

Second, leaders should smell like sheep. In their leadership style—whether prophet or pastor—their hearts should be enrobed with shepherd's garb.

After His resurrection, Jesus had an intriguing lakeside chat with Peter on the shores of the Sea of Galilee (see John

21:15–23). Three times the Lord asked Peter if he loved Him. Jesus' query here was not just an incidental conversation thrown in for color in John's gospel. The time between Christ's resurrection and ascension was of critical import, and we would expect the Holy Spirit to record those stories and teachings that summarized much of Christ's ministry. And this story is given a lot of copy!

When Jesus asked Peter if he loved Him, Peter demurred a bit, couching his response in words that were friendly but noncommittal. Jesus laid out for Peter the measure of the love He was looking for: "If you love Me, you will feed My sheep."

Reading between the lines, I think the Lord Jesus was trying to recalibrate Peter. It was almost as if Jesus was saying to Peter, "When I send My Holy Spirit and the Church is birthed, you will become the most visible leader among your peers. When that happens, Peter, I want you to remember this: I don't want you to be seduced by the power that comes with leadership. I want you always to remember that in My Kingdom 'feedership' comes before 'leadership.'"

Jesus was awakening Peter to the dangers of pride laced within the calling of leadership. He wanted Peter to understand that the shepherd was the basic model for leadership in His order of things. The shepherd tends the sheep, which means that a shepherd's leadership is not expressed in a straight line, accomplishing task after task, goal after goal. The shepherd's leadership is defined by the needs of the sheep. The shepherd will go anywhere to get green pasture and fresh water. There is a sort of meandering quality about the shepherd-leader.

Feeding sheep is a somewhat directionless endeavor. Growth in such an enterprise is measured primarily by whether those sheep are coming into wholeness (nothing to write newsletters about, necessarily). But Jesus commissioned His first leaders in this way, and it strongly suggests the MO of His kingdom.

With this background, consider these passages on leadership:

> The overseer must be above reproach as God's steward . . . holding fast the faithful word which is in accordance with the teaching, so that he will be able both to exhort in sound doctrine and to refute those who contradict.
>
> Titus 1:7, 9, NASB

> Prescribe and teach these things. . . . Give attention to the public reading of Scripture, to exhortation and teaching.
>
> 1 Timothy 4:11, 13, NASB

The action to note here is the ministry of feeding. Before leaders were called to build churches, take cities and launch ministries, they were called to *feed people.* Again—"feedership," *then* leadership.

By placing the emphasis on "feedership," the Lord underscored the way success is measured in His kingdom. It is easy for us as leaders to find ourselves driven by the goals we set for our ministry and for the church or organization we serve. The push to meet those goals imperceptibly creeps into our hearts, and we find ourselves exhibiting controlling behaviors. We become frustrated, irritated, testy. Without realizing it, meeting our goals becomes intertwined with who we are, our identity.

For the "feeder-leader," goals are not the determinants of his identity; they are merely *measurements of obedience.*

Goals are important, but only in that Jesus gives them to us. It is not that goal-setting is wrong; goal-setting is simply part of the process of following Jesus. And His ways are not our ways. Oftentimes He does not give us the "big picture" we want. Instead, He gives us just enough revelation to spur us on, but not so much as to make us less dependent on Him. Arbitrarily setting goals for what we think is a good cause, even a God-given one, may seem like good stewardship. But in reality it can be a subtle snare of pride. Even something as constructive as goal-setting can be a means of attempting to control our future through overplanning.

The call to "feedership" over "leadership" places the control of the growth process squarely in Christ's hands. Agendas are pursued and goals are realized as believers come into a full-faced relationship with the Lord.

Leaders as Confirmers

Third, a leader should perceive his role as a confirmer of God's promises. Paul writes about himself in this way in 2 Corinthians 1:20. Here Paul encourages the Corinthians that "no matter how many promises God has made, they are 'Yes' in Christ. And so through him the 'Amen' is spoken by us to the glory of God." This passage is one of the most clarifying definitions of leadership in the New Testament. Paul reminds the Corinthians that the God who makes the promises fulfills those promises through Christ. What kinds of promises might Paul have had in mind? The promises of blessing, guidance, security, peace. And what Paul is also saying is that these needs are met not by him as a leader, but by Christ. It is almost as if Paul is saying, "Don't look to me for your guidance, or your sense of security, or your sense of significance. I am not the 'Yes,' but just the 'Amen.'"

There is a critical boundary marker here. Paul knew that he was not the one to procure these benefits for the Corinthians. He was simply called to model how Christ guided him, provided for him, led him in security. They were to be nourished not by what Paul provided for them but by what he modeled for them. Ultimately they were to discover how Christ met *their* needs by considering how Christ met *Paul's* needs.

Paul was not the "Yes"—he was just the "Amen." This does not mean that we, as leaders, become dispassionate observers, standing on the sidelines cheering on our flocks. We are not just coaches; as we will see in the next section, leaders are to be spiritual fathers and mothers as well. And in that sense we do provide unflinching commitment to those under our leadership. Still, the best thing we can provide for them is our model of Christ's faithfulness.

Many leaders nobly want to serve well. But in their earnestness they can cross a line where they try to be the "Yes." Some leaders actually like the sense of control they feel when people look to them for guidance and security. Of course, most leaders do not possess such Messianic complexes but are simply trying to serve effectively. However noble the motive, leaders can, in their zeal, inadvertently portray themselves as the provider. And that is why so many leaders burn out. God never called us to be the "Yes"—just the "Amen."

If we as leaders continue to try to be the "Yes" when we are called only to be the "Amen," we may find ourselves not only burning out but crossing lines of pride that can substantially minimize our effectiveness.

Leaders as Connectors

A fourth perception, which highlights the importance of leadership while staying faithful to the idea of the priesthood of all believers, is to view leaders as connectors. We know that the analogy of the body was Paul's favorite when it came to describing how the Church was to function. Drawing on this analogy, what member of the body might correspond most closely to the function of a leader? The eye? The mouth?

Ephesians 4:12 might give us a hint: "To prepare God's people for works of service, so that the body of Christ may be built up." Perhaps it is best to view leaders as the "joints" in the body. They are the wrists, the elbows, the kneecaps. They are the ones who connect the rest of the members. They are the ones who facilitate movement for the whole body. Even the neck is a joint, although I think the neck—through which the Head's communication passes—might be better understood as the Holy Spirit's function. All in all, I think that "joint" best captures the critical importance of leadership (for without the ability to move, a body soon dies) without perpetuating an inappropriate hierarchy, which would only widen the gap between clergy and laity.

Leaders as Parents

Fifth, the role of a "parent" is a primary template for any spiritual leader. In fact, Robert Banks makes the case that the Church as God's "household" is a more important metaphor for Paul than the Church as Christ's "body."[1] In describing the Church, Paul uses the "body" picture to convey mutual ministry and the "household" imagery to capture community. Since God is the Father of the household, our leadership "parenting" can be framed as accountable stewarding of God's family.

I like what my friend Larry Kreider says:

> Being a father is not something you *do*, as much as it is something you *are*. . . . A spiritual father is always a servant first. Paul called himself a father several times in Scripture, but he uses the word "father" to denote not *authority* but *affection*; therefore, he calls [the Corinthians, in 1 Corinthians 4:14] not his *obliged*, but his *beloved* sons.[2]

Leaders as Releasers

The sixth picture of healthy leadership needs some introducing. Even the best of leaders can become control freaks. Second Corinthians, the letter that contains Paul's discussion of the "Yes" and the "Amen," also notes in chapter 3 that Moses, after speaking with the Lord, would put a veil on his face in order to prevent the Israelites from gazing at his face while the radiance of God's glory was fading away. Why? One wonders if it may not be due to the fact that Moses secretly needed to stay in control, to maintain his place of authority, to reinforce his position of influence. One wonders, perhaps, if this subtle desire to control was not the root of his disobedience at Meribah. It was there that Moses struck the rock, though God had said simply to speak to it, and cried, "Listen, you rebels, must we bring you water out of this rock?" (Numbers 20:10). It was that "we" (Moses and Aaron) that betrayed Moses' true motivation for which he was judged. The hidden tumor of control had metastasized into a cancerous pride that ultimately cost him his chance to enter the Promised Land.

Paul goes on to say in 2 Corinthians 3:14–18 that the Holy Spirit wants our faces unveiled. He so wants leaders to know freedom from having to assert control, the liberty simply to contemplate the glory of the Lord and allow their ministry to be the overflow of their communion! So many in leadership today are weighed down with excess baggage because they are carrying loads they were never intended to carry, assuming authority they were never intended to assume. And for many the motive is not necessarily one of pride, but of a genuine desire to please Christ. Moses maintained his veil not because of blatant pride, but rather because it seemed so necessary. But oh how those necessary things can begin to dictate our "responsibilities"—until we find ourselves controlled by "control."

The sixth image to consider, then, is the opposite of being a *controlling* leader. It is the image of being a *releasing* leader, a "palms-up" leader—one who no longer has to hold on to his or her authority to feel validated in his or her leadership.

The Descending Stairwell

Whenever we as leaders try to "possess" authority, we invariably begin to "control"—control our lives, our relationships, our future. Like Adam, when we assume control we have taken on a role for which we were not designed. Therefore our identity, who we really are, becomes clouded. In our desperate search for our identity we turn to what we *can* control—our "ministry." The freedom to be unveiled before His glory is lost and we are left to find ourselves in terms of ourselves. Our sense of worth no longer comes from our relationship with Jesus. Instead, we start deriving our identity from what we do. In some, this stirs an inordinate drive for success; in others, it prompts an unbearable pressure to maintain success.

Once we have crossed this line we begin to compromise our integrity. Attaching our identity to our ministry, we begin walking down a descending stairwell into deception.

- We begin making choices from opportunistic motives, choosing on the basis of what will advance our career or enhance our reputation.
- We start estimating a person's worth in terms of talent and ability, not character. The pressure to maintain success has caused many a leader to delegate responsibilities to those of unsound character.
- Need becomes the criteria for ministry. We do things and start programs in order to satisfy the demands of parishioners or to remain competitive with other churches.
- Our preaching becomes more of a tool to motivate than an opportunity to feed.
- We find ourselves planning events and projects to create a sense of momentum rather than in response to the will of the Lord.
- Even our desires for revival become based on the need for spiritual stimulus to spur the people to meet our own numerical quotas and ministerial goals.

Once our integrity has been compromised, the flow of spiritual life is choked. The Word becomes a tool whereby we manufacture messages rather than God's love letter by which we commune with Him. Our gatherings become events to motivate people rather than to celebrate Jesus. While our motives do not always outright deteriorate, they do become mixed at best.

As our sense of inner authority wanes, we begin to look to people for affirmation of our ministry, and our convictions become diluted by their opinions. We are moved by the success of others, rather than by the Spirit of God. Grasping for recognition, we cease to be prophetic. As Tony Campolo has observed, it is impossible to be prophetic and hold a position of power at the same time.

Viewing ourselves in terms of talents, titles and tasks, we cease to be authentic. Instead of the great "oaks of righteousness" Isaiah spoke of (Isaiah 61:3), we look more like creeping vines—quickly growing and covering ground. But we find ourselves to be a million miles wide and only a half-inch deep. We become obsessed by our direction, rather than possessed by a daily passion for God! We become visionaries, not commissioned servants . . . all because of the seduction of power and our feverish desire for control.

Leaders Who Glorify God

Typically we think of glorifying God as praising Him for what He has done in our lives. In a sense, we think of glorifying God as giving Him the credit for what we do. Though this sounds pretty noble, I do not think this gets to the crux of what glorifying God means. I suggest that it is a matter of giving Him not the *credit* for what we do, but the *control* of who we are. God does not want the credit; He wants control! For if He has the control, He will get the credit! We must always remember that the government is to be "on His shoulders."

The heart's hidden quest for power may be hard to detect, but it does manifest itself in the bent to control. To keep from becoming controlling leaders we need to do two things. First, we need to retrace our steps and view the whole idea of "leadership" through the lens of God's character and nature. Second, we need to see where we have wrested the control from Jesus, asking ourselves five key questions:

1. Is what I am doing as a leader promoting an environment where we as a church or ministry are daily experiencing the active headship—the "control," if you will—of Jesus?
2. Are those under my care more connected to Jesus than to me?
3. Does our ministry culture reflect the character of Jesus? His joy, peace and rest? His determination against the enemy, His patience with the unlovely, His freedom from people-pressure?
4. Am I finding myself having to prod the ministry along—constantly motivating or entertaining the flock to stay envisioned about our programs and direction? Have I remembered that those things "birthed" by God generally grow because of the inherent life within them, without needing my constant stimulation?
5. Do our programs and ministries enhance relationship-building and mutual interdependence? Are people feeling empowered? Have I remembered that Jesus builds His work through the process of building relationships

precisely because our relationships, and how we tend them, comprise the aspect of our lives least apt to be controlled by others?

Conclusion

When it comes down to it, the real antidote to control is humility. We still come back to the bottom line of spiritual brokenness. A leader who handles authority well exhibits the characteristics of brokenness. An Anglican bishop, John Collinson, once described what spiritual brokenness is. It still all comes back to this:

Sometimes it is asked what we mean by brokenness. Brokenness is not easy to define, but can clearly be seen in the reactions of Jesus, especially as he approached the cross and in his crucifixion. I think it can be applied personally in this way:

When to do the will of God means that even my Christian brothers will not understand, and I remember that "neither did his brethren believe in Him" (John 7:5), and I bow my head to obey and accept the misunderstanding, this is brokenness.

When I am misrepresented or deliberately misinterpreted, and I remember Jesus was falsely accused and that he "held his peace," and I bow my head to accept the accusation without trying to justify myself—this is brokenness.

When another is preferred before me, and I am deliberately passed over, and I remember that they cried, "Away with this man, and release to us Barabbas" (Luke 23:18), and I bow my head and accept rejection, this is brokenness.

When my plans are brushed aside, and I see the work
of years brought to ruin by the ambition of others, and I
remember that Jesus allowed them to lead him away to cru-
cify him, and he accepted that place of failure, and I bow
my head and accept the injustice without bitterness, this is
brokenness.[3]

16

The "Control" Factor

Put two or three men in positions of conflicting authority.
This will force them to work at loggerheads, allowing you
to be the ultimate arbiter.

Franklin Roosevelt

Mahatma Gandhi was once asked what he would do first if
he was given unlimited power to bring any positive change
to the world. His response was unhesitating: "I would find
someplace where I could rid myself of that power."

Most spiritual leaders are not power brokers. They would
not traffic in political chicanery or stoop to Machiavel-
lian techniques to get ahead. But where the seductiveness
of power can ensnare the spiritual leader is in tempting
him to control. The yen to control is a much more subtle

expression of power, because often the desire to control can spring from seemingly innocent motives—like ensuring the quality of a program or seeing that parishioners are pleased. But the itch to control can be a fine web of pride that over time traps a leader in a lifestyle of drivenness and anxiety, which can bring great harm to those around him.

How can we as leaders handle authority in a way that nurtures within us a noncontrolling style of leadership? The manner in which a leader handles authority is perhaps the single most important factor in creating an environment in which people can readily align themselves to authority, and thus come into greater freedom. So how should a leader carry authority?

He will let his example motivate others' desire to follow.

In other words, he will allow his personal lifestyle to elicit naturally in others a desire to submit to his leadership. He will not demand it.

Submission to authority is an important measure of true humility. The issue here is not so much the rightness of submission, but rather how it is summoned. The great danger is the tendency for leaders to demand submission in the name of discipleship. But the emphasis should never be the leader's *demand* for submission, but rather the disciple's *need* to submit. Maturity comes, in part, as we submit to those authorities God puts in our lives—but we who are in a place of God-given authority ought not to demand submission from others. A young believer may desire to submit to you. Let him desire it, and teach him what he desires, but do not grasp for his following.

Submission to authority is like the sexual relationship within marriage. Physical intimacy is absolutely necessary in a marriage, but make it necessary and you destroy its dynamic! The same with submission. Submission is vital, but let's not take an observed truth and make it a law that kills.

When submission is cultivated in a follower by watching a leader's example, the follower will not feel manipulated or controlled. The leader who does not demand submission is a leader who is not threatened when his authority is questioned. The nondemanding leader creates an environment in which people can question, because he wants them to cultivate obedience out of personal conviction—not fear of a leader's displeasure. And if his authority *is* challenged, and rebellious attitudes *are* identified, the servant-leader deals with such attitudes, even if aggressively, from the standpoint of rescuing the insubordinate from their own folly.

Is there cause to respond firmly to protect the flock from divisive conduct? Yes, but I suggest that ought to be a secondary motive. Act first to restore the believer; then act to protect the flock. Remember, God's anger is always expressed as a means of preservation. We must, as leaders, resist the rancor within when someone's behavior threatens our agenda. The noncontrolling leader lets the truth of submission be discovered within the follower rather than demanding it of the follower.

He allows trust to set the boundaries of authority.

The leader does not try to extend his authority beyond the trust that has already been established. For example, a parent may extend to me that measure of trust that allows me to speak into the way he raises his kids, but not necessarily the way he handles his finances. If I assume that his extension of trust in one area is a carte blanche that authorizes me to intrude in all areas, I may inadvertently come off as controlling.

Floyd McClung says, "Biblical authority is never taken; it is offered." McClung goes on to say that our actions should proceed "from an attitude of equality, not authority, because [we should be] more concerned with serving than ruling."[1] This is true whether we are parents, pastors or presidents.

He receives and expresses confrontation well.

One who handles authority well is one who can receive and dispense correction in the spirit of gentleness. Confrontation is not easy for any of us, because in confronting someone we risk rejection. But our reluctance to go there is rooted in the fear of man. We do not want to confront because we are too concerned about what others think of us.

We must be willing to incur someone's disfavor for the sake of right convictions. This does not mean that we have to be rigid or stubborn. It just means that a person who understands authority also understands the importance of boundaries, and therefore sees the value of reinforcing those boundaries with proper correction—whether they be directed to him or to those with whom he interacts. It also means that he will quickly champion that which is right, even in the face of human opposition. In short, it means that he is willing for people to not like him—which is, after all, an issue of moral courage. Proverbs 27:6 says, "Faithful are the wounds of a friend" (NASB). The sincerity and depth of a relationship is in part measured by an honesty genuine enough to say lovingly what is wrong. My aunt, Billy Sue, once told me, "I'd rather hurt your feelings than hurt your future."

Peter is an instructive example of a leader who responds well to confrontation. In Galatians 2:11–21, Paul recounts the story of his encounter with Peter when he had to rebuke him during Peter's visit to Antioch. Peter was clearly in the wrong, but it must have stung to have the upstart apostle Paul upbraid *him*, the one who had been, after all, the primary leader at the Church's inception. But apparently Peter received this correction with grace and maturity, since we find Peter, in his own letters, responding to Paul in a gracious manner. We can draw much from Peter's example.

First, Peter was not reluctant to receive from Paul. In his first letter, Peter gratefully acknowledges the help of Silas, whom he regarded as a faithful brother (see 1 Peter 5:12). Silas, as we know, was Paul's companion for a season. It would have been quite likely that Silas drew from the well of Paul's influence as he interacted with Peter in later years—and Peter is grateful for the exchange. Second, Peter not only acknowledges Paul's wisdom in 2 Peter 3:15, he specifically acknowledges his authority, citing Paul's important apologetic concerning the thorny issue of the apparent delay of Christ's second coming. Third, Peter seems to embrace Paul emotionally when he refers to him, in the same verse, as his "dear brother."

There is no hint of offense in Peter. Obviously Peter had received Paul's combative overture years before with humility and grace—and now was drawing on an inner reservoir of magnanimity toward Paul as he sought to guide his flock. Such a leader can be trusted, because he receives correction graciously.

He is not threatened by conflict or apparent failure.

The story in Acts 6 about the overlooked widows is important not just for the fact that it shows us how the early Church handled conflict, but also because it shows how the apostles responded to what essentially was a criticism of how they were leading the church. There are, of course, many layers to this. The apostles could have succumbed to the fear of man and pandered to the legitimate interests of their constituency. Legitimate though they were, had the apostles responded in such a way it would have introduced a consumer mindset into the Church that would have compromised it down the road. It is also notable that conflict became the backdrop and staging ground for the birth of a new ministry group, the deacons. This should encourage us to see conflict in a more constructive way—as a stimulant for possibility rather than as a threat to our security.

There is another aspect to this discord. The apostles do not seem threatened by or insecure from what could be seen as a referendum on their leadership. They were not afraid to consider that their administrative weakness may have contributed to the tension, nor do they blanch at what appears to be a failure on their part. A hint as to why they responded so securely may be found in their response, as they aver, in essence, "We should not give ourselves to waiting on tables but to prayer and the ministry of the Word." This revealed that their sense of value was measured not by what they did but by their relationship with God, which is defined by prayer and the ministry of the Word. When a leader responds in this way, it frees him—not to ignore the conflict or explain it away, but rather to embrace it in order to see what God is doing.

He knows that authority is determined by how relationships are cared for.

Wise leaders know that their authority is legitimized to the degree that they nurture their relationships. The Kingdom of God, as we know, is the *rule* of God. His rule flows from who He is. And who He is, is perfect community. Therefore, rulership flows from relationship.

Near the end of His life, Jesus refereed a rather heated debate among His disciples. They were wondering which of them possessed the "right stuff" for greatness. Jesus cut right to the chase and said, "The greatest among you should be like the youngest, and the one who rules like the one who serves" (Luke 22:26).

Immediate impressions from this comparison come to mind. Younger people tend to defer to others. They hold older people in high esteem. They listen and learn. They relate to others out of their innocence rather than out of their experience. (Well, that is the theory anyway.)

What Jesus is saying is that these are the kinds of people who are the greatest. And we can easily see why. How would you and I respond to someone from whom we felt high respect, who wanted our opinions, who listened more than talked, who was never manipulating in his dealings with us? We would follow!

He allows the Spirit's anointing on him to maintain his authority, rather than asserting it himself.

The Bible is clear that there are gifts of leadership given to the Body and that we are to obey those in leadership. The author of Hebrews exhorts, "Obey those who rule over you" (Hebrews 13:17, NKJV), and then includes in his closing words, "Greet all those who rule over you" (verse 24, NKJV). But I suggest that the intent of such statements is not to reinforce chains of command, but rather to call us to be sensitive to our leaders because of their accountability to God. Hebrews 13:17 goes on to call for submission to "those who rule over you" because "they watch out for your souls, as those who must give account" (NKJV).

The emphasis is not on the spiritual leader's right to receive obedience, but on the sobering truth that kingdom rulership is delegated by God and is therefore maintained by God's anointing—not by man's politics. Because of the weighty implications of their accountability before God, leaders are not to concern themselves with *leadership* so much as they are to concern themselves with *obedience*.

A cursory glance at the word *rule* in the New Testament substantiates again the truth that, rather than being a stepping-stone to leadership, servanthood *is* our leadership. Let's look at a couple of examples.

In 1 Timothy 5:17 we read, "The elders who rule well are to be considered worthy of double honor" (NASB). The word for *rule* in this verse is *proistemi*, meaning "to stand before, to preside, to practice." This same Greek word is used similarly in Romans 12:8 and 1 Thessalonians 5:12. It is interesting, however, that *proistemi* is translated "maintain" in Titus 3:8 and 3:14: ". . . be careful to maintain good works . . . learn to maintain good works" (NKJV). Putting these passages together, one gets the sense that *proistemi* has to do with ruling through good works or ruling through servanthood!

In Hebrews 13:17, the word for "rule" is *hegeomai*, meaning "to lead, to command with official authority, to judge, to have the rule over." Yet this is the word Jesus uses when

He says that "the one who rules [*hegeomai*]" is to be like "the one who serves" (Luke 22:26). Here Jesus identifies the kind of delegated authority received from God. It is first a *charismatic* authority and second a *positional* authority—in other words, an authority primarily derived from character and anointing, not position. *Hegeomai* is a word that synchronizes nicely with the shepherding imagery that is to characterize the godly leader, for it can also be translated "to guide, to lead by giving counsel."

He allows ministries under his care to emerge from the bottom up rather than to be designed from the top down.

A good leader desires to see ministries born as people mature and discover their gifts and callings. In a culture that prizes the can-do visionary, it is easy for us to slide into predictable patterns where the leader, as spiritual entrepreneur, forges an agenda, sets his goals, then seeks to mobilize his followers behind his vision. Most leaders are sincere in their attempts to receive such visions from God, and in many cases these ideas are God-inspired. But, again, there is a fine line between serving people by envisioning them and using them to facilitate our aspirations. How can we encourage ministry development in a way that harmonizes with Christ's headship?

First, launching ministries and birthing visions through the process of believers discovering their gifts puts the control of vision squarely in the hands of the Holy Spirit. It calls the leader to rely on Jesus and what He wants to initiate in His time. For example, as a pastor I may have a deep desire to launch a ministry to the local university. But what happens if in the process of nurturing those under my care the first person who matures into his calling has a burden for the homeless? If I am allowing Jesus to rule, I will recognize what He is birthing and support it—whether or not it is high on my personal agenda. This does not mean that I stop praying for our university, nor does it mean that I discontinue voicing my causes and convictions. It does mean that I honor Jesus by giving place to those who hear His call, whatever it is, and who possess the commensurate maturity to lead out in their ministry.

Second, no matter how pure-hearted the visionary or how stellar the visions he receives from God, he is still only one individual. There is just so much vision that even the most broad-minded leader can accommodate emotionally. At some point he simply cannot muster adequate enthusiasm for everyone's ministry. People who rise to ministries that do not register on the leader's radar often feel disconnected, lost or unimportant. They then become vulnerable to resentment, feeling that the leader does not care. To limit the boundaries of ministry to what the leader can envision puts undue stress on the leader, risks disappointing at least some people and ultimately detracts from the active presence of Jesus in the life of the body of believers.

So what does the noncontrolling leader do? Disengage his visionary gears? Shift into neutral? That would be to deny some of the essential qualities that make him or her a leader in the first place!

How can a leader who has genuinely received vision from God nurse that vision along? If it is from God, that leader is mandated to marshal those under his care to follow it. Again, how can he confidently lead out in a way that squares with Christ's headship? Here we can segue into a final point.

He initiates ministries in a way that fosters dependence on Christ, not on his leadership.

Let's say a pastor gets an idea from God to start a worship band. He is excited, of course, because he knows this will create an outlet for the musicians as well as inspire the congregation. Many visionary leaders would take the approach of stirring the people from the pulpit, motivating them through newsletters and the weekly bulletin, exciting them about what a worship band could do to enhance congregational life. After a month's campaign, signing eager musicians to the roster, he appoints someone to lead the endeavor, calls their first rehearsal and launches the band. And things go well . . . for a while. Until the first rift occurs—differences of opinion between band members or grumbling over the amount of rehearsal needed to pull off an effective worship set. Soon the congregation begins to feel the tension in the air.

What is the pastor to do? His "charisma" set the vision in motion. But now, faced with fraying nerves and dissatisfied parishioners, he confronts one of the laws of leadership: *He who starts the ministry has to sustain the ministry.*

Multiply this scenario over time throughout several departments, and soon that buoyant visionary either has been worn out in his efforts to maintain visionary momentum or has become increasingly edgy and curt in his leadership style. Followers become disillusioned with leaders, and leaders become disillusioned in their calling—longing for simpler days when opportunities were seized, church life was innocent and their communion with God was uncluttered.

So what would Jesus do?

Let's consider the same situation from a different angle. The leader gets the vision from God. But he wants to see it "birthed" in a way consistent with Christ's headship. The first thing he does is pray. Conception takes place only in the place of intimacy. If Jesus wants to birth something, He will impregnate our hearts with the seeds of vision as we wait on Him in worship and prayer.

Once the leader feels a peace from God to do so, he begins to share the vision through expanding circles of influence. He begins with his closest inner circle, depending on how global the vision is: perhaps the elders of the church, perhaps his executive staff. He spends time—weeks, maybe months, depending on the vision—letting them pray about it, digest it, own it.

After a while he goes to the next circle, perhaps the other boards—the deacons or trustees—and the rest of the pastoral staff, repeating the process. Why? Because he wants Jesus to be in control of the procedure and he knows that Jesus is *most* in control through the process of building trusting relationships. Since he is dealing with visions that will affect the whole of the fellowship, wisely he will want to share in successive circles of authority, beginning with the group that exercises most authority related to the particular vision being considered. This way visions are not prematurely shared with the various leadership groups, and certainly not with the congregation as a whole, thus minimizing the potential of defrauding the fellowship by promoting visions and ministries before proper foundations have been laid.

While he is laying the foundations of leadership support for the vision he feels God is summoning them to, he begins to teach the congregation biblical truths supporting that particular vision, without yet announcing the vision. In our example, perhaps he spends time teaching on the strategic role musicians and Levites played during King David's reign.

By the time a thorough biblical foundation has been laid and the vision has been absorbed by several layers of leadership, it can be proclaimed publicly.

If our objective is to give God maximum glory by allowing Christ's headship to be experienced, then how does this seemingly laborious process accomplish these objectives?

First, by allowing the vision to be digested by growing circles of influence we are allowing the project to grow by relationship. As we have seen, the arena of relationships is the arena we are least likely to control, which forces us to depend on the Spirit's power to impact people with the vision. Again, the more dependent we are, the more Christ is in control; and the more Christ is in control, the more God is glorified.

Second, by laying a biblical groundwork for the vision, the leader is allowing the people to respond to it out of spiritual conviction rather than his enthusiasm. In allowing people to respond to the Word, they are responding to Jesus—rather than to the leader's motivational panache. Again, God is glorified, because the people are more intimately connected to Christ.

In our efforts to direct people toward meaningful objectives, we as leaders often use the familiar adage, drawn from Proverbs 29:18, "Without a vision, the people perish." It is true, of course, that people want to be led somewhere; it is also true that one of the functions of leadership is to discern God's direction for the people. However, in the name of effective leadership we can cross a certain line and begin to use this principle as a means of corralling people behind our particular pursuits. We reason that if we are the leaders God has placed in a given situation, then our visions are the important ones behind which we must mobilize the followers. Without meaning to do so, we see the flock as components in the accomplishment of our dreams. If the people do not measure up to our expectations, we as leaders can soon find ourselves impatient and driven.

Yet in the original language, Proverbs 29:18 does not have to do so much with human enterprise as it does with fresh revelations of God! This verse is better read, "Without a fresh vision of God, the people perish." This is that for which God's children long! This is that from which, when we lack it, we perish!

A Life Let Go

It is true for all of us, and especially for a leader: The greatest salvation Jesus offers is salvation from ourselves. For when we try to control our lives, our ministries, our world, we inevitably become controlled by that very drive. The leader who has let go is the leader who can let grow—let those around him, those under him, as well as himself, grow into the fullness of Christ.

17

The Ultimate Issue

Every aware, conscious, sentient spirit is divine and has
direct access to truth. . . . Open source embodies that. There
is no authority.

> Dan Kriegman, founder of Yoism, a new, "open source"
> religion that operates and evolves over the Internet

Not too long ago a high schooler was caught cheating on
a test in school. The violation was blatant and the consequences very clear. And yet this student had the audacity
to turn around and sue the school district for allowing an
environment in which he could cheat! That is absolutely
ludicrous—but it shows how distorted right and wrong have
become in society, as well as how concepts of authority can
so easily be twisted to fit the situation. It echoes the ancient

prophet's description of the final end of a rebellious society: They "call evil good and good evil" (Isaiah 5:20).

Over the centuries, humankind's rebellion has ripened. Now we have cultivated a culture in which authority is something to be questioned, resisted, tolerated—but not embraced. And in so doing we have also developed a society in which we have become the most "schizophrenic" of people. And this schizophrenia is a picture of just how bound we are.

We are incomplete—but demand our independence.

There are only two kinds of beings that can be truly happy. The first kind is one who is complete and independent. By "complete" I mean that such a being would know everything and would thus be secure in that independence. The only being who fits this description is God. The second kind of being who can be truly happy is one who is incomplete—because such a being would *not* know everything—and thus, by definition, is dependent.

The absurdity of fallen humanity is that we want it both ways. Though we do not know everything, and are thus fundamentally incomplete, we still want to be independent. Logically, this is an impossible way to live. Yet we resist yielding to God's authority and acknowledging our dependence on Him. Consequently, in demanding our independence we will find ourselves inwardly conflicted.

The idea of the autonomous, independent individual is illusory. It is a fantasy clutched by postmoderns to buffer the harsh reality that, adrift from God, we are alone and needy.

Fantasy produces bizarre behaviors. When I was young, I fantasized about being Superman. I would run around the neighborhood with a bath towel pinned to the back of my collar. Cute maybe, but had I persisted in the fantasy as a grown man I soon would have been met by the little men in white coats.

The point is that unreality soon leads to aberrant behavior and illogical thinking. The insistence, for example, that embryonic stem cells are the best way forward to finding cures to diseases—when the evidence clearly points to the fact that *adult* stem cells are more than adequate and that we do not have to rely on abortions in order to harvest embryonic stem cells—shows how skewed our thinking can become just to maintain our "individual rights." Is it logical to kill the unborn in the name of saving the diseased when we have a better alternative anyway? But to disallow the right to an abortion is to accept a "fence" to our independence. And that is what really galls the postmodern secularist.

We crave community—but demand autonomy.

Our confliction is poignantly seen in our culture, where the yearning for genuine community is pitched to the aching point. The feeling of being nothing more than a bit of datum on some cosmic computer screen gnaws at postmodern humanity. Yet we who crave community cannot truly find community because we will not let go of our treasured autonomy. We are addicted to independence. Because we are misaligned to divine authority, we assert our self-sufficiency. We want to be absolutely free and independent to do what we want to do when we want to do it—and the world be damned if anybody gets in our way. But it is this very demand that keeps us from valuing a healthy sense of dependence, which in turn fosters genuine community.

We want to feel secure—but refuse to believe in absolutes.

This, too, is a commentary on how conflicted we are. Because our postmodern culture has landed squarely on the side of relativism—that ultimate truth is unknowable and that the only truth that can be known is what is true to each individual—we are now consigned to perpetual insecurity. We are insecure because we can never really know what is absolute truth, or if absolute truth even exists. The irony is that we would rather live in our insecurity and hold on to our individuality than hold out for the possibility that there *is* universal truth and that it *can* be discerned. To admit that there is universal truth is to obligate us to an authority outside of ourselves. Hence our aversion to authority is making us more and more insecure as people, *and we would rather be riddled with anxiety than to let go of our autonomy.*

In her book *Total Truth*, Nancy Pearcey shows how relativism doubles back on itself in a logical absurdity. Specifically addressing evolutionary psychology, which holds that ideas themselves are products of evolution and therefore are in constant relativistic flux, she concludes, "If all ideas are products of evolution, and not really true but only useful, then evolution *itself* is not true either. And why should the rest of us pay it any attention?"[1]

Evolutionary psychology is just another genie out of the same bottle of relativism that has hung around for generations.

And relativism is simply man's insistence that he will not accept any other boundaries except his own independent mind. He *will* be the measure of all things, even if it leads him to the edges of insanity.

We want community—but disregard covenant.

The Puritans knew that a right understanding of authority produces genuine community, because they understood the inseparability of authority and covenant. To *covenant* was to yield to the authority that comes when we give our word for something; it is to yield to the authority of the community. It was to place the concerns for the community, and the sense of duty that comes with that, ahead of one's own preferences.

The concept of "covenant," while at times being a code word for control in some circles, is a concept that has fallen out of favor in our culture. But in many ways understanding covenant is the way back to rectifying the root wrong of independence. And this is another part of our schizophrenia: We want commitment but we eschew covenant. The hyper-individualism that marks 21st-century life is evidence that we have not understood authority.

We want justice—but refuse to believe in absolute right and wrong.

At the very root of our moral crisis, and every other crisis for that matter, is this issue of refusing to see things in terms of right and wrong. A recent book ridicules the President and defines his "tragic legacy" by finding fault with him for framing the issues of the world in terms of right and wrong. But unless there *is* right and wrong, we have no foundation on which to erect a system of justice. We are left with a legal whimsy that all too often creates a vacuum of power and in which no standard can serve as a guard against injustice.

Yet we have no other course *but* to frame issues in terms of right and wrong. Francis Collins—one of the most respected scientists of our day, the head of the Human Genome Project, and a committed Christian—points out just how illogical relativism can be in his book *The Language of God*. Speaking of the "Moral Law" written on every person's heart, he states:

> That the Moral Law exists is in serious conflict with the current postmodern philosophy, which argues that there are no absolute right or wrongs, and that all ethical decisions are relative. This view . . . faces a series of logical Catch-22's. If there is no absolute truth, can postmodernism itself be true? Indeed, if there is no right or wrong, then there is no reason to argue for the discipline of ethics in the first place.[2]

We want global harmony—but dismiss universal morality.

Because postmodern culture refuses to adhere to any possibility of universal authority, we find ourselves with yet another schizophrenia: a desire for harmony while at the same time eschewing the idea of absolute moral truth—which is a critical component of that harmony. Unity works only if there is a reference point of authority that ties us together.

It may appear logical to believe that because nobody has the complete picture, absolute truth can never be fully known. But this flies in the face of reason as well.

The fact that we possess an innate desire for community shows that we must also innately believe in the possibility that enough "common standards" exist for community to be realized. If this is true locally, why not also hold that there is a universal morality that can nurture unity on a global scale? If we dismiss the concept of universal morality as religious totalitarianism, then who decides when we have enough morality that we agree on to construct *any* community? By resisting the authority of some universal code beyond ourselves, we are actually dooming ourselves to alienation.

A society that overthrows the boundaries of authority opens the door to absurdity. The very commodities and values we desire—community, safety, justice, security, happiness—are no longer attainable. Only when we abandon our resistance to authority will we be free of our social schizophrenia. To be truly happy, to be genuinely free, to be actually safe, we must go back to the root issue—our bent to act independently of God—and realign to His authority. This is true freedom, not only for ourselves but for our world.

Notes

Chapter 1: The Root of All Wrong

1. "Mario Savio," Wikipedia, http://en.wikipedia.org/wiki/Mario_Savio.
2. Watchman Nee, *Spiritual Authority*, trans. Stephen Kaung (New York: Christian Fellowship Publishers, 1972), 11.
3. James Waldroop and Timothy Butler, "Managing Away Bad Habits," *Harvard Business Review on Developing Leaders* (Boston: Harvard Business School Press, 2004), 26.

Chapter 2: Getting It Right

1. Duke University, "Nagging Spouse? You May Have an Excuse for Not Responding," *ScienceDaily*, February 14, 2007, http://www.sciencedaily.com /releases /2007/02/070213142855.htm.

Chapter 3: Authority—Another Word for Love

1. The phrase "led by the Spirit" (Romans 8:14) is in the passive voice, meaning that the Holy Spirit is at work in us and this is not according to our own energy. Yet the phrase "put to death the misdeeds of the body" (Romans 8:13) does refer to some action on our part, so that it can be said that there is something palpably felt of the Holy Spirit that registers within a human spirit in a sensory way. Because of their bias against the supernatural, some commentators fail to draw the appropriate connections here.
2. Paul Billheimer, *Destined for the Throne: A New Look at the Bride of Christ* (Fort Washington, Penn.: Christian Literature Crusade, 1975), 33ff.

Notes

Chapter 5: The Source of Authority

1. Quoted in Alister E. McGrath, ed., *The Christian Theology Reader* (Oxford: Blackwell, 1995), 110.

2. The early Church fathers thought the Trinity of God to be the hinge upon which the preaching of the Gospel turned. Thomas F. Torrance's opening statement in his book *Trinitarian Perspectives* (Edinburgh: T & T Clark, 1999) captures what ought to be the pulsating rhythm of Christian theology in *every* generation: "The doctrine of the Trinity has been called the innermost heart of the Christian Faith, the central dogma of classical Christianity, the fundamental grammar of our knowledge of God" (p. 2).

3. For example, Athanasius and Gregory of Nazianzus.

4. For example, Irenaeus and Basil of Caesarea.

5. Leonardo Boff, *Trinity and Society*, Liberation and Theology Series, no. 2, trans. Paul Burns (London: Burns and Oates, 1988), 120.

Chapter 6: How God Models Authority

1. Stanley Milgram, "The Perils of Obedience," *Harper's Magazine*, 1974.

2. James MacGregor Burns discusses this in his Pulitzer Prize–winning book *Leadership* (New York: Harper & Row, 1978), 24.

3. It is important to realize that Paul *does* use this term in the context of "authority over" as well—as in the husband-wife relationship—but even there it is intertwined with this idea of head as "source of life," which greatly shapes the way authority is expressed. We will discuss this more thoroughly in a later chapter.

4. J. Robert Clinton, *The Making of a Leader* (Colorado Springs: NavPress, 1988), 197.

Chapter 7: Bridled by the Spirit (Humility on the Inside)

1. Ken Gire, *Windows of the Soul: Experiencing God in New Ways* (Grand Rapids: Zondervan, 1996), 44.

2. A. W. Tozer, *The Set of the Sail* (Camp Hill, Penn.: Christian Publications, 1986), 17, italics added.

Chapter 8: Bucking Our Boundaries

1. Paul Billheimer, *Love Covers: A Viable Platform for Christian Unity* (Fort Washington, Penn.: Christian Literature Crusade, 1981), 110.

2. R. T. Kendall, *Tithing: Discover the Freedom of Biblical Giving* (Grand Rapids: Zondervan, 1983), 27.

Chapter 9: Sanded to Fit (Authority and Community)

1. Owen Chadwick, ed., *Western Asceticism* (Philadelphia: Westminster Press, 1958), 159.

2. David A. Heenan and Warren Bennis, *Co-Leadership: The Power of Great Partnerships* (New York: John Wiley & Sons, 1999), 101ff.

Notes

Chapter 11: The Five Basics of Authority

1. Steve Fry, *I Am: The Unveiling of God* (Sisters, Ore.: Multnomah, 2000), 137–38.

Chapter 12: The "S" Word

1. In Ephesians 5:22, the Greek word translated by the English word "submit" is *hupotasso*, meaning, literally, "to arrange under." In Paul's time, this word was used as a military term. It was also used with reference to the behavior of a servant to his master (Fritz Rienecker and Cleon Rogers, *Linguistic Key to the Greek New Testament* [Grand Rapids: Zondervan, 1976], 538). It can also mean "subordinate" (F. Wilbur Gingrich, *Shorter Lexicon of the Greek New Testament* [Chicago: University of Chicago Press, 1971], 208). It "demands readiness to renounce one's own will for the sake of others . . . and to give precedence to others" (Gerhard Kittel, ed., *Theological Dictionary of the New Testament* [Grand Rapids: Eerdmans, 1978], 8:45). The primary usage of the word *hupotasso* emphasizes the relationship of a follower to a leader.

2. Fawn Parish, *The Power of Honor: Learning to Love Well* (Camarillo, Calif.: Conversations Publishing, 2007).

Chapter 15: The Palms-Up Leader

1. Robert J. Banks, *Paul's Idea of Community: The Early House Churches in Their Cultural Setting* (Peabody, Mass.: Hendrickson Publishers, 1994), 49.

2. Larry Kreider, *The Cry for Spiritual Fathers and Mothers: Compelling Vision for Authentic, Nurturing Relationships within Today's Church* (Ephrata, Penn.: House to House Publications, 2000), 35, italics in original.

3. John Collinson, "What Brokenness Is," a pamphlet printed by Calvary Fellowship Mission, Little Smoky, Alberta, Canada.

Chapter 16: The "Control" Factor

1. Floyd McClung, *The Father Heart of God* (Eugene, Ore.: Harvest House, 1985), 129–32.

Chapter 17: The Ultimate Issue

1. Nancy Pearcey, *Total Truth: Liberating Christianity from Its Cultural Captivity*, Study Guide Edition (Wheaton: Crossway, 2005), 217.

2. Francis Collins, *The Language of God: A Scientist Presents Evidence for Belief* (New York: Free Press, 2006), 24.

Steven Fry is the president of Messenger Fellowship (www
.messengerfellowship.com), a network of leaders and
churches committed to reformation in the Church and
transformation in the nations. He also serves as lead pastor of The Gate, a nondenominational church in Franklin,
Tennessee (www.thegatenashville.org).

As a pastor, author, composer and recording artist, Steve
blends worship and scriptural teaching in a way that is relevant and revelatory. He is known widely for penning such
songs as "Oh, I Want to Know You More" and "Oh, the Glory
of Your Presence" and the critically acclaimed musicals *We
Are Called* and *Thy Kingdom Come*. He has traveled the globe
speaking at churches, conferences and leadership seminars.
He is the author of a number of books, including the popular
I Am: The Unveiling of God and *Rekindled Flame*.

Steve received his master's degree in theology from the
Wesley Institute and the Sydney College of Divinity. He has
served as a board member of many local and national ministries and has recently become the president of the International Worship Institute (www.worshipinstitute.com).

Steve and his wife, Nancy, have three children and live in
Brentwood, Tennessee.

Awaken the Passion...
Restore the Message

Steven Fry is the president of Messenger Fellowship, a community of leaders and churches committed to modeling and multiplying "presence-shaped" paradigms of ministry. Steven is also involved in many forms of creative communications, and his life message aspires to awaken in people a passion for God and to summon the Church to align with the Kingdom. As a pastor, author, composer and recording artist, Steve blends worship and scriptural teaching in a way that is both relevant and revelatory.

More books by Steven Fry:
I Am
Rekindle the Flame
Safe in the Father's Arms

To order, or for more information, visit www.stevenfryministries.com